Ethical Governance in Health Care

Ethical Governance in Health Care

A Board Leadership Guide for Building an Ethical Culture

Roger A. Ritvo, Ph.D.
Joel D. Ohlsen, M.D.
Thomas P. Holland, Ph.D.

Foreword by Sr. Mary Roch Rocklage, RSM

Health Forum, Inc.
An American Hospital Association Company
CHICAGO

Printed in the United States of America—10/04

Cover design by Cheryl Kusek

ISBN: 1-55648-320-1

Item Number: 196147

Discounts on bulk quantities of books published by Health Forum, Inc., are available to professional associations, special marketers, educators, trainers, and others. For details and discount information, contact Health Forum, Inc., One North Franklin, 28th Floor, Chicago, IL 60606-3421 (Phone: 1-800-242-2626).

Library of Congress Cataloging-in-Publication Data

Ritvo, Roger A.
    Ethical governance in health care : a board leadership guide for building an ethical culture
/ Roger A. Ritvo, Joel D. Ohlsen, Thomas P. Holland ; foreword by Sr. Mary Roch Rocklage.
    p. cm.
    Includes index.
    ISBN 1-55648-320-1
      1. Health services administration—Moral and ethical aspects. 2. Health
facilities—Administration—Moral and ethical aspects. 3. Hospital trustees. 4. Medical
ethics. I. Ohlsen, Joel D. II. Holland, Thomas P. III. Title.
    RA427.25.R55 2004
    174.2—dc22   2004056833

To my parents, Mikki and Mike Ritvo,
whose professional commitments and community service
exemplified the values of this volume.—*Roger A. Ritvo*

To my mother, Dorothy Ohlsen,
and to my mentor, Dr. J. Robert Stewart,
who each provided rock-solid grounding in ethical
decision making.—*Joel D. Ohlsen*

To Steve and Eleanor Blackmon, my parents-in-law,
who have demonstrated so well how to be wise
and responsible community leaders.—*Thomas P. Holland*

And to the thousands of trustees
who provide guidance and stability
to our hospitals and health care systems
and who have taught us many important lessons.

Contents

List of Figures

List of Cases for Discussion

About the Authors

Roger A. Ritvo, Ph.D., serves as professor and vice chancellor at Auburn University Montgomery (Alabama). His previous position was dean and professor at the University of New Hampshire's School of Health and Human Services. Other positions have included director, graduate program in health administration, at Cleveland State University, as well as senior policy adviser to two secretaries of the U.S. Department of Health and Human Services. Dr. Ritvo received his Ph.D. from Case Western Reserve University and his M.B.A. in health services administration from George Washington University. The American Hospital Association published his collaborative book *Improving Board Effectiveness* in 1997. He has also co-edited *Managing in the Age of Change*. His most recent book, *Sisters in Sorrow,* presents the biographies of women who labored in the Nazi concentration camps as nurses and doctors serving fellow prisoners.

Joel D. Ohlsen, M.D., a radiation oncologist, is director of cancer services for St. Mary–Corwin Medical Center in Pueblo, Colorado. Dr. Ohlsen has served on its board of trustees for more than fifteen years, has been a member of the American Hospital Association's Regional Policy Board (Region 8) for seven years, and is a member of the AHA Committee on Governance. In addition, he is a member of the board of trustees of the Colorado Health and Hospital Association, and he is the chairman of the board of the Sangre de Cristo Hospice. Dr. Ohlsen has led discussions with trustees across the country regarding the role of hospital trustees and the challenges they are facing.

Thomas P. Holland, Ph.D., is professor and codirector of the Institute for Nonprofit Organizations at the University of Georgia. He holds a doctorate from Brandeis University, where his research focused on the impacts of management changes on staff members and consumers. For more than thirty years, Dr. Holland has taught graduate courses in the management of nonprofit organizations, and he has conducted extensive research on their governing boards. He consults with boards internationally and has written numerous publications on governance. Dr. Holland is the lead author of *Improving Board Effectiveness,* published by the American Hospital Association in 1997.

Foreword

E*thical Governance in Health Care* is an effective guide for the development of boards, a useful orientation tool for new board members, and an invaluable resource for ongoing education and self-evaluation. The authors have achieved their objective of providing "a pathway toward the goal of effective, accountable governance within an ethical framework." In addition, they accentuate this information by providing case studies and excellent questions to stimulate discussion.

The book demonstrates that governance itself is the pathway for fulfilling the mission of the health care enterprise. It is important to note that the pathway never really ends—it is a continuum. Those serving in governance must make decisions that are consistent with the core identity and values of the institutions they serve. Doing this with integrity and in an ethical manner is the meaning of responsible governing.

What is most heartening about this book is the continual emphasis on the most important role of governance: to ensure that the mission of the health care enterprise is the foundation for all the decisions that are made. In order to make decisions that will ensure fidelity to the mission, those serving in governance must clearly enunciate and serve in accordance with the values and guiding principles of the organization. It is important that each time the board meets, members reorient themselves to the mission and guiding principles of the organization for which they are stewards and make their decisions accordingly—not based on their personal preferences.

The decision-making process can be more important to ethical governance than the actual decision being made. If the process takes place in accordance with the institution's guiding principles, the outcome will be a decision that is faithful to the mission of the organization. Effective decision-making processes take into account the larger community served, as well as the stakeholders, physicians, coworkers, patients/clients, and interests of the institution. Focusing on these areas provides a disciplined approach to ensuring that all viewpoints and concerns are brought to the table. The final decision should always be tested against the mission and guiding principles of the organization to make sure the decision makers are true to its values.

While reading *Ethical Governance in Health Care,* I was reminded of a book written by James Collins and Jerry Porras, *Built to Last.* It states that enterprises that are built to last know and live by their core ideology, which includes their purpose and acts as their guiding star. Further, there are few values and principles that should ever be violated for any short-term advantage or financial gain. These are the same concepts explained in *Ethical Governance in Health Care.*

Ethical governance in health care demands commitment and fidelity. Those who have been given the ability to serve in governance have accepted this authority, thereby creating their own personal responsibility to make decisions in accordance with their institution's mission and guiding principles. *Ethical Governance in Health Care* provides valuable information for anyone who is charged with this obligation and teaches how to make decisions in keeping with the spirit and values of an organization.

I wish all who read this book peace and blessings on the ethical journey of health care governance.

Sr. Mary Roch Rocklage, RSM
Chair, Sponsor Council
Sisters of Mercy Health System
St. Louis, Missouri

Past Chairperson, Board of Trustees
American Hospital Association

Acknowledgments

THIS BOOK would not have been possible without the help of many colleagues, friends, and supporters. While writing is ultimately a process that takes the authors' time and energy, successful manuscripts result from the input of so many others. We are grateful to the following people for their guidance, exhortations, and feedback.

Thousands of trustees over the years have helped us formulate our thinking. Their service makes the U.S. health care system reach its current levels of excellence. Through training programs, trustee development seminars, and responses to our previous books and articles, members of numerous boards have individually and collectively focused our work and stimulated our creativity by sharing their good ideas, experiences, and reflections.

Our editor at AHA Press, Richard Hill, knew the value of this topic and asked us to meet the challenges of these contemporary issues. We appreciate Rick's guidance and constructive feedback throughout the process.

Andrew Pasternack at Jossey-Bass supported this project and helped immeasurably in shaping the book's goals.

Evan G. DeRenzo, Ph.D., a bioethicist at the Center for Ethics, Washington Hospital Center, Washington, D.C., greatly assisted with earlier drafts of this work.

Janie Singletary, a student assistant, prepared the manuscript in a professional manner, almost always with a smile.

Rachel Helms, another student assistant, completed the numerous edits in an orderly fashion.

Mandy Erickson, a freelance editor, provided excellent editorial suggestions that organized the material and made the book easier to read.

Any errors or omissions remain our responsibility, and we regret not finding them before publication.

Ethical Governance in Health Care

1

Being Effective in a Changing World

HEALTHSOUTH. WorldCom. Tyco. USAir. Arthur Andersen. These corporate giants have become symbols of greed, deception, criminal activities, and civil liabilities. And each has a board of directors that did not know what was happening, chose to ignore the signs of danger, or actively approved actions that have led to international scandal.

It is an easy stretch to connect these headlines to the health care sectors. A prominent philanthropist in Cleveland once discontinued all donations to local charitable organizations, including health facilities, until the trustees of these organizations pressured the trustees of Case Western Reserve University to reform their board.

As this volume goes to press, lawsuits continue to unfold against the trustees and officers of the now-bankrupt Allegheny Health Education and Research Foundation. Insurers and creditors are suing trustees of this once huge nonprofit health care system in Pennsylvania, charging that trustees failed to exercise appropriate oversight of the CEO's actions or to avoid conflicts of interest between board members and the system. Not only is the organization now defunct; these suits also seek compensation from individual trustees.[1]

The public has a right to demand accountability. The nation's health care and medical system should continue internal reform because intrinsically it is needed, and extrinsically it will preclude government and legal intervention. This book provides a pathway toward effective, accountable governance within an ethical framework.

Many contemporary observers of the governing boards of nonprofit organizations present critical, and probably accurate,

1

indictments of their effectiveness. A 1996 article in the *Harvard Business Review* begins with the following sentence: "Effective governance by the board of a non-profit organization is a rare and unnatural act." It continues, "Non-profit boards are often little more than a collection of high-powered people engaged in low-level activities."[2]

Experience in the health sector makes this generalization seem accurate. There are too many egregious actions and mistakes directly attributable to lax oversight and weak governance. But this scathing evaluation of nonprofit governing boards, and by extension its trustees, does not have to predict failure. Rather, it should be a wake-up call to trustees and CEOs to design programs and allocate resources that will develop the skills of board members.

The health care landscape is full of other examples of ineffective governance, some of them in premier academic medical centers. The hospitals and medical centers affiliated with Duke University, the University of Colorado, the University of Pennsylvania, the Johns Hopkins University, and the University of Chicago are just a few of the hospitals that have been sanctioned by the federal government. When trustees fail to oversee ethical compliance and regulations, the consequences are both real and symbolic. A 2003 essay in the *Chronicle of Higher Education*, "When Good Institutions Behave Badly," refers to these situations and clearly illustrates why this volume is necessary.[3]

Boards of trustees must collaborate with institutional leaders to respond to the changing legal, moral, and ethical climate of the health care system. As the ultimate responsible entity, trustees create, sustain, and oversee the management and operations of the health care institution and provider-patient relationship. Quality and public confidence must not be allowed to erode any further. This was dramatically emphasized in March 2004 by the U.S. Court of Appeals for the Seventh Circuit in a ruling that stated: "If the hospital cannot shield its . . . patients' records from disclosure in judicial proceedings, the hospital will lose the confidence of its patients, and persons with sensitive medical conditions may be inclined to turn elsewhere for treatment."[4]

Organizational Ethics

The field of organizational ethics—including its history—helps us understand the ethical implications for health care organizations. Of course, there is no single event or date to which we can point as the beginning of organizational ethics. Rather, it draws from several interconnected sources. For example, the Joint Commission on Accreditation of Healthcare Organizations (JCAHO) has helped to focus attention on the field and its implications for patient care providers. Issues began to take form through the self-study and site-visit peer review process. We know, however, that meeting the JCAHO standards and criteria does not ensure the ethical treatment of patients, nor does it guarantee that an organization is ethical.

The field of business ethics took form and substance from the consumer movements of the 1960s and 1970s. The ancient saying *caveat emptor* ("let the buyer beware") had been the mantra for decades and was complemented by the slogan "What's good for General Motors is good for the country." This spirit of corporate needs taking precedence over individual rights was challenged in the social upheaval of the 1960s. The infamous Ford Pinto, a vehicle with a safety-related defect in the design of its fuel system, became a rallying point for social activists. So too the Tuskegee experiments, in which the American public learned that individual health care providers were violating ethical standards of the medical profession and federal regulations.

Social movements can change health care practices. Thus, boards need to be aware of such external shifts in the surrounding environment and how they might affect board decisions.

Understanding the Environment

Health care organizations face a changing environment, one in which patients expect more care while insurers struggle to balance employer demands for cost containment with seemingly uncontrolled rises in expenditures. This is an era in which the term *cost containment* has come to mean less service, more delays, and the anonymous voices of policy reviewers who make treatment decisions. These trends show no sign of abatement in recent studies documenting the growth of managed care. Hospital mergers are now as common as those in the corporate sector. Indeed, health care stocks now have their own financial index. It would seem that profitability is almost as important as patient recovery.

The Moral Compass

Current events challenge our assumptions daily. How can boards work effectively when public expectations change so rapidly? How can boards respond to contemporary moral challenges such as those raised by Dr. Kevorkian's actions in assisted suicide? Hospital presidents and insurance company executives find their compensation packages under the public microscope, even though many of their industrial counterparts make more than they do. We do have a different set of societal expectations for health-related institutions, and these expectations turn our moral and ethical compass in new directions. As the field of organizational ethics grows, it becomes imperative for effective governance to include these elements in its decision process.

The Hospice Movement

One contemporary element poses special challenges for health care providers and systems. Board members must be conversant not only with the hospice movement as a social phenomenon (albeit not a new one) but also with what this movement means for the decisions to be made by providers and patients. Patients who once were obvious candidates for surgery or chemotherapy now may opt for a different approach to the end of life. These decisions have an immediate and profound effect on the medical care given by the staff; that is obvious. But these decisions present new challenges to the board as well. The decision to *treat, operate, or medicate* now yields to *allowing the patient to self-medicate, making the patient comfortable, and directing the transfer to a long-term care facility or home care agency.* Often the immediate response of the board is to ask the lawyers for advice. This is a good idea but only as a starting point. The attorney can relate the law(s) but not the strategic implications for the board.

Balancing Margin and Mission

"It's a mess." These words came from the director of New Mexico's Agency on Aging in testimony to a state legislative hearing on the numerous elderly without health insurance. The cause of this turmoil has become all too familiar in the health care landscape. Four of New Mexico's largest health maintenance organizations (HMOs) announced plans in the summer of 2000 to drop more than fifteen thousand Medicare patients from coverage.[5] Obviously, this created a tidal wave of anxiety throughout the senior citizen community as well as within the state's health care facilities.

Three health care providers in Mobile, Alabama, decided in concert to "stop treating Bay Health Plan patients, citing lack of payment."[6] Such actions would have a direct (and negative) impact on twenty thousand Medicaid-eligible recipients. Similar stories appear across the nation as the demand for cost containment intersects with the increasing cost of providing care. At the same time, state legislators and corporate financial officers raise concerns about the inexorable rise in health-related expenditures. The result of such pressures in the political system and in organization boards makes headlines in Albuquerque, Mobile, and elsewhere. The poor, the elderly, and those without a group voice often suffer the consequences.

Patient Expectations

While such large-scale, group-level exclusions receive national attention, individual patients struggle daily to receive the services they need and their physicians prescribe but services the insurance company questions. This puts health providers in the unenviable position of being caught between the patient's needs and reimbursement. As a response, Louisiana's state legislature developed a new entity called the Medical Necessity Review Organization.[7] Partially because of the federal umbrella protection against most lawsuits, states are developing alternative mechanisms to hold HMOs accountable for their actions. When care is deemed a necessity, the HMO would be compelled to pay for services. Current congressional deliberations propose to force HMOs to accept low-income enrollees.

Many health care experts and institutional leaders worry about the impact of changes in federal reimbursements. These concerns are about more than just the bottom line—they concern the misuse of facilities. When low government payments lead to patients' lack of access to physicians, compelling them to use the emergency room as their primary access to care, expensive facilities become crowded with nonemergencies. This results in a direct financial cost and, consequently, a social cost. Is it possible that we entered the first years of the twenty-first century struggling with the same issues that dominated national conversations in the 1970s, the 1980s, and the 1990s? The recent downsizing of home health departments has exacerbated the situation, as fewer community-based providers are available to see indigent patients. Lower federal reimbursements will lead to longer patient stays when patients come in with more serious, but untreated, illnesses.

These trends have a direct effect on how health care institutions are managed and governed. In the boardroom and the operating suite, difficult choices must be made. How the institution defines its options will indelibly alter its service profile, its personality, its culture, and its reputation. Attempts to move from a model of paternalism (the doctor knows best!) to a more patient-centered model have forced the paradigm in other directions. Law, insurance policies, corporate demands, public policy, and societal attitudes now stress individual (patient) autonomy—the idea that each of us, when informed, can make our own responsible choices.

Furthermore, there has been an explosion of information available to patients. Now patients expect certain levels of competence, quality, and care from their providers. Because of the public's approval of the role of the JCAHO, patients expect a professional care staff that is qualified, competent, unimpaired, and without conflicts of interest. These same patients expect institutional systems to ensure confidentiality and an accurate, retrievable medical record.

Managed Care

Years ago, managed care was heralded as the best way to gain control of the nation's rising health care costs; it was attractive in its infancy because of its stress on prevention and early intervention. Yet the managed care system in the beginning of the twenty-first century bears no relationship to the promise of its early years. It has developed a reputation for ineffective care, delayed treatment, impersonal service, and the infamous voice on the 800 telephone number denying coverage. The problem is fundamental to the manner in which managed care has evolved.

Historically, the patient-provider relationship was paramount, and medical ethics centered on patient rights, informed consent, and reasonable provider and patient expectations. There was little interference with the doctor-patient interaction. That fundamental principle endured for centuries, but it has changed in our lifetime. Indeed, it changed in the last twenty-five years. Physicians have found their practices engaged in the incremental but inevitable transformation from private practice to corporate employee. In many situations, a fixed contract for services defines in advance which services are covered and which are not. Obviously, the problem arises in treatments that the provider feels are appropriate but that the contract excludes. In fact, this creates one of the most potentially egregious situations: a physician's income may increase because of services not rendered and monies not spent.

This takes us full circle, back to an era before managed care. The fee-for-service system was decried because it seemed to encourage physicians and institutions to provide as much service as they could in order to maximize revenue. Under managed care, these same individuals and institutions may increase their revenues by not providing services, tests, and treatments. Delayed visits save money.

As providers find themselves on compensation contracts that have incentives for increased profit sharing, will their professional judgment be clouded? Even if this does not happen, there is an appearance that it may, raising the concern that a provider may not be acting solely in the patient's best interests. Rather than linked to a medical work ethic, personal income is tied to less work.

The federal government has a long, rather distinguished history of helping communities and hospitals through the Hill-Burton Act, which was passed a generation ago. One of the act's underlying principles is that community hospitals have an obligation to provide care for those in need. Uncompensated care is often the only way many people can access today's health care system. Initially, proprietary health care systems were criticized for creaming the best patients (meaning the easiest to treat or those who could afford services) and leaving the indigent and more difficult cases to others. Such social cost shifting did, or did not, occur—depending on whom one chooses to believe.

Issues with managed care have assumed a new poignancy since some of the HMOs have gone out of business, become subject to corporate mergers, or ceased to exist through buyouts. In 1999, one of the industry's (note the word *industry,* not *sector*) oldest HMOs decided to pull out of the northeastern United States. Kaiser Permanente reached this decision reluctantly, but the HMO found that its practices, market penetration, and care principles did not meet the competitive demands of that region.

There is little that employers or public regulators can do to force an HMO to stay in business beyond the term of its contractual obligations. In fact, the leaders of most HMOs in such situations argue that patient care is exactly the reason for their decision to pull out, merge, or sell. In order to keep services and costs within reasonable limits for their *subscribers* (not *patients*), the HMOs must stop serving others. It is the business ethic at work, and the stock market will respond positively for these courageous acts. But what about the institutions, providers, patients, and subscribers who counted on the HMOs?

Issues for the Board

Nonprofit boards have a special role in applying these external trends to the hospitals they are charged to govern. To understand this role, some background is in order. Boards arose out of the desire to support and sustain private action for public good. This desire typically has two components: accomplishing some purpose in a community (such as providing health care for sick and injured people) and preventing the power and resources dedicated to that purpose from passing into the hands of the state.[8] Trustees of organizations created on such grounds are engaged in work that is based on the principles of sustaining fiduciary responsibility and serving the common good.

The fiduciary foundation of governing boards is composed of the related roles of entrusters, trustees, and beneficiaries. The entrusters, or founders, are people who identify the community goal and arrange for the resources to carry that out. The founders transfer responsibility for guiding the organized pursuit of the goal to trustees, who are charged with carrying out the intentions of the founders for the good of the intended beneficiaries or recipients of services. The trustees' actions are bounded by the prior relationship with the founders and the purpose for which the organization was established.

Governance is grounded in loyalty to the vision and intentions with which an organization was created. The founders want to ensure that their vision for some form of benefit to others extends beyond their own lifetime. Rather than relying on the public sector to do that, they invite others to help by means of a private organization that will continue after they are gone. These collaborators are not elected representatives or delegates of the beneficiaries, although they have an obligation to listen, respect, and attend to current community concerns. Nor are they simply agents carrying out specific orders of the founders, though the vision and purposes of concern to the founders are central to their decisions.

In addition to loyalty to the purposes for which an organization was created, boards must deal with the likelihood that founders may have had multiple, possibly even contradictory, intentions and strategies based on their cultural context and available knowledge. Furthermore, community needs and resources change over time, making interpretation and reinterpretation of original intentions crucial in the work of the board. Likewise, no organization can address every need of every possible beneficiary or stakeholder. The board must decide how best to use limited resources in ways that address some specific aspects of the common good and do so in ways that promote justice and integrity.

Eventually, every board comes up against conflicting interests, whether these involve differences among members over how best to adapt programs to circumstances the founders did not foresee, how to make the best use of limited resources, or which organizational or community needs will be served and which postponed or ignored. Within the context of the general values of the society in which they live—including honesty, fairness, and respect for others—board members have to make difficult decisions about what the organization will and will not do and directions it will and will not take. The moral worthiness of the organization's purposes and directions, as well as the means by which they will be carried out, should be weighed regularly by the board to ensure that they are fair to all, consistent, and sustainable and that they continue to serve the common good.

Trying to remain faithful to the original intentions of the founders while being respectful of current beneficiaries and community needs can pull a board in opposing directions. Focusing exclusively on the former can lead to stagnation and irrelevance in the face of new perceptions, emerging insights, and new technology. Focusing only on the latter pulls an organization in multiple directions without any consistent vision or clear grounds for allocating resources. To reconcile these forces, the board must serve as an interpreter, linking the original vision with new needs in ways that guide current decisions about resources and priorities and ensuring that the organization is faithful both to the founders and to the community. The board stands as the bridge between founders and beneficiaries, reconciling differences among them.

Judgments about organizational purposes and priorities can be extremely difficult, and trustees should recognize and address the conflicts among multiple interests. Revisiting the organization's mission statement is crucial for staying loyal to the intentions of the founders in considering the present needs of the community and the interests of staff members. Such discussions can best be held within a cohesive, reflective group that is well aware of the history of the organization, present circumstances and resources, and likely future trends. The boardroom should be the place where different interpretations of the organization's purposes are reconciled with the current needs of the community. Board members must work with those who have a stake in the organization's current and future work, including staff members, patients and their families, current and prospective donors and beneficiaries, and community leaders.

Although understanding these multiple interests is vital to making informed decisions, at the same time the board must maintain some objectivity by keeping a respectful distance from those interests. The boardroom is the place where all the many commitments and interests bearing on the organization are addressed and conclusions reached. It is the place where value differences, complex problems, and uncertainties about right directions can be voiced; it is the place where alternative conclusions are thrashed out with candor and trust.

In sum, the board is called on to remain faithful to the vision of the founders, serve the well-being of the community, and interpret the past to guide meaningful decisions about the present and future. These principles should guide the board in its decisions and plans. They will not prevent differences or conflicts in meetings; indeed, disagreements will occur. Handled respectfully, however, such differences can lead to fresh and creative conclusions that strengthen decisions and improve the whole organization.

How This Book Is Organized

This book addresses the challenges to actively redefine the role, function, power, and process of governing boards. Chapter 2, "Developing Skills in Ethical Analysis," presents an overview of the major frameworks for ethical analysis. As a practical guide, chapter 2 helps trustees understand different perspectives in confronting moral and ethical dilemmas. Then, when hard choices must be made, trustees will be able to use appropriate frameworks for explanation and justification. If the board lacks moral and ethical authority in its own work, there is little likelihood that the system will support its ethical posture. When patients or staff members assert that the institution is more concerned about cost than care, it is a clear sign that the board needs to work on its own ethical practices.

Chapter 3, "Creating the Ethical Organization," defines the difference between the legal environment and a facility's ethical climate. Trustees are the custodians of the organization's identity and must translate its values into future plans and actions. The organization's services require ongoing attention to ensure they justly reconcile past commitments with present and future needs. Using case studies to stimulate the reader's imagination, some guidelines for effective practice emerge.

Chapter 4, "Implementing the Hospital's Mission," deals with the most critical issue of putting mission into practice. At stake is the hospital's ability to build and maintain the trust of the community, staff members, insurance companies, public regulators, and accreditation agencies. An effective governance process establishes an ethical climate and culture that continually bring out the best in the organization's personnel. All members of the internal organizational community need to understand the importance of moral choices and how to increase self-awareness about their own moral filters.

Chapter 5, "Exercising Ethical Leadership," focuses on how boards can respond to select issues that challenge most organizations. Chief among these are conflicts of interest. Although actual conflicts may be rare, the *appearance* of conflict causes suspicion and a lack of trust. Boards must be diligent in this regard. It takes years to build a community's trust and only a few days to lose it. Conflicts of interest cause so many problems that they require a special place in this volume. Trustees must move beyond minimum compliance. Examples from several different perspectives illustrate contemporary issues confronting many boards; these include relationships with the pharmaceutical industry, advertising, and managed care.

Chapter 6, "Conclusions and Actions," brings together the themes in this book. It provides keys for effective, ethical governance. After all, that is why health care boards were created and what our society expects of them, today and tomorrow.

Case studies on relevant issues in American health care offer a basis for discussion and are provided throughout the book. These cases focus our attention on how boards can establish policies that by default enhance or impede high-quality care and institutional morality. Often these issues end up in an ethics committee or under the purview of individuals engaged in the morbidity and mortality review process. However, when risk management and legal experts enter the conversation, the conversation changes. We therefore exhort trustees to become more active participants in these activities. It will inform them and enlighten health care delivery personnel about the consequences of trustee actions.

The For-Profit Specter

The Columbia/HCA saga of the late 1990s, in which the business practices of a large, for-profit hospital chain were the focus of a federal investigation, has raised the issue of for-profit versus nonprofit health care. Less than a generation ago, offering health and medical services for profit was anathema to institutions with core values of care and service. Many providers and policymakers believed it was a fringe activity, generally relegated to the margins of delivery systems. Maybe it was, or maybe these proprietary facilities and services were a portent of the future.

Nevertheless, the for-profit model is here today and is likely to continue as a major component of our health care delivery system. Managed care, public policy, and the corporate model have altered the traditional provider-patient relationship. There are two major ethical issues raised by these pervasive systems of care.

The first issue: the *price* of care to the patient is distinct from the *cost* of that care. The fading fee-for-service model encouraged more care, more tests, longer stays, more visits, and less attention to cost. In times past, the more care that was given, the more the revenue the hospital or provider would receive. Now, these costs are microscopically monitored. But the price charged to the patient or the insurance company includes a profit. In the nonprofit world, this surplus reverts to the organization for reinvestment in services and education, and this is an integral part of the system's mission.

The second ethical issue: the traditional market approach to health care is now defined at the bargaining table between the leaders of the provider organization and the insurance company

negotiators. Lost in this negotiation are the poor, a special con-
stituency for nonprofit providers. Managed care excludes them for
the most part. This leads to a recurring charge that for-profit hospitals take the cream, choosing to serve those patients who can afford
to pay and from whom they can make a profit. If true, this would
leave the more complex, costly, and intensive cases to the public and
nonprofit hospitals. On the other hand, proprietary hospitals pay
taxes that the public sector can use to offer care for the indigent. The
for-profit sector, using sound data, notes that many nonprofit hospitals have closed, leaving inner cities with fewer facilities to serve a
low-income population. This is the crux of a major public policy
dilemma.

We hope this volume will stimulate trustees and directors of
both private and public, profit and nonprofit health care organizations to reach the goal of effective, accountable governance within
a solid ethical framework. Ethical issues may vary by location, ownership, and institutional complexity. But a constant theme remains:
governing boards have a job to do, and that role has largely been
forgotten or overlooked until recently. Keep these points in mind as
you read this book and accept its challenges.

References

1. L. R. Burns, J. Cacciamance, J. Clemant, and W. Aquino, "The Fall of
   the House of AHERF: The Allegheny Bankruptcy," *Health Affairs* 19,
   no. 1 (January 2000): 7–41.
2. B. Taylor, R. Chait, and T. Holland, "The New Work of the Non-
   Profit Board," *Harvard Business Review*, September/October 1996:
   36–46.
3. T. E. Murphy, "When Good Institutions Behave Badly," *Chronicle of
   Higher Education*, 19 December 2003: B15.
4. A. Johnson, *Montgomery Advertiser*, 27 March 2004: A2.
5. *The New Mexican*, 3 August 2000: A1.
6. *Mobile Register*, 28 August 1999: A1.
7. *The Times Picayune*, 29 August 1999: F1.
8. D. H. Smith, *Entrusted: The Moral Responsibilities of Trusteeship*
   (Bloomington, Ind.: Indiana University Press, 1995).

2

Developing Skills in Ethical Analysis

THE FIELD of health care ethics has focused largely on individual patient or provider concerns such as informed consent, confidentiality, autonomy, and malfeasance. However, the policy implications of medical ethics have caused many to wonder whether the public sector has made appropriate decisions. In the United States, we really do *ration* medical services without ever using that term. It is not politically acceptable to acknowledge that as a society we choose not to meet and pay for some people's health care needs. The role of the courts and the government do have an impact on how our systems operate.

As the trustees of Sibley Hospital in Washington, D.C., learned years ago, there are serious legal, ethical, and organizational consequences when fiduciary responsibilities are neglected. In this case, case law expanded the concept of fiduciary responsibility so that trustees could be legally liable for conflicts of interest. Although 1974 may seem like ancient history in light of the issues confronting today's health care system, some themes remain constant. Everett A. Johnson, Ph.D., a leading authority of that time, wrote an article, "The Practicing Physician's Role in Hospital Management—An Administrator's View."[1] At that time, his proposal was somewhat controversial: the administration and the medical staff must "work together . . . in a sense of confidence and willingness to have judgments challenged. . . . No board can operate on the notion that 51 percent of the votes cast is a reasonable way to lead effectively; the board must reach consensus." This wisdom remains true today. It is also a guide for ethical decision making.

Three fields converge to form the core of health care organizational ethics: individual ethics, corporate ethics, and institutional ethics. The early work on individual ethics led to corporate ethics. Now that government and financial concerns have entered the national and international debate about the allocation of health care resources, the emerging conversation centers on institutional ethics.

Individual ethics focuses on individual acts, agents, decisions, and consent. Institutional ethics includes public policy and legal issues. The mediating societal structure between these two is the organization. Thus, the social institutions of the family, professional associations, and managed care components must reconcile the needs of the individual patient/client and hospital within the limitations of public policy, law, and regulations.

The emergence of managed care in the past several decades has made it clear that clinical ethics cannot be separated from the way the clinical component is organized and the way its legal, financial, and policy systems work. Ethical issues are beyond the control of any one institution. Now, ethics assumes a different paradigm in that it examines what is the social good. In order to look at this dimension, it is necessary to ask the following questions: Do institutions have a conscience? Is there a culture of ethical decision making at the organizational level? Or are organizational cultures only the sum of the individual decisions? It is our belief that there is, and must be, a corporate ethic.

Health care organizations lie between individual and social mores and expectations. This is the locus for most medical transactions. Which ethical principles accrue to the institution from the policies of our society and the characteristics of the changing doctor-patient relationship? Boards of trustees are the major structural link to the communities outside the hospital walls. Their legal mandate as fiduciaries captures the concept, but ethical obligations extend beyond that. The board of trustees must ensure that the public learns about the critical choices every institution makes as a regular part of its business operations.

Health care institutions are not autonomous systems. Their choices are made in an environment where employers define most health insurance coverage in this country outside of government programs, and a growing number of our population do not have health insurance. This reality constrains any hospital in meeting the expectations of the numerous constituencies it serves. How can these opposing forces, often on a collision course, be reconciled?

Educating the various constituents—potential patients, organizational leaders, political representatives, and other health care providers—has become a critical requirement of effective board governance. The board and the institutional leaders are accountable for acting ethically in their decisions, which are almost always under public scrutiny. This is not controversial. What is controversial is the nature of these decisions, given the conflicting goals and the numerous constituencies to be served. To reach the goal of ethical decision making, a broad cross section of hospital staff members, community advocates, and policymakers must be actively involved.

The federal Sarbanes-Oxley Act of 2002 sets high standards of accountability for corporations and their boards. Although these standards have not yet been applied to nonprofits, many experts believe they will be used as standards for public assessment of such organizations, especially those that issue tax-exempt bonds.[2] Health care board members can compare their practices with those standards and determine what changes they can make that will put them ahead of the curve.

Competencies for Effective Ethical Decisions

Effective governing boards have internal systems that allow them to model best practices of organizational effectiveness. Effective boards use six competencies to ensure continued quality improvement and ongoing success. These have been defined in the literature and can be used by board members willing to devote the time to improve processes. *Improving Board Effectiveness,* a book by Thomas Holland, Roger Ritvo, and Anthony Kovner, defines these clearly and describes easy-to-use instruments.[3] The six competencies are contextual, strategic, educational, analytical, political, and interpersonal. These are described briefly below.

Contextual competencies help trustees become aware of the issues, problems, histories, and ideals facing the larger society as well as their institution. These provide the background against which contemporary decisions must be made. Ethics are larger than any one organization; trustees must understand the environment in which they function. The changes over time concerning advertising are illustrative: Is such commercialism an ethical practice involving patient education, or is it just marketplace competition?

Building on these skills, boards must have strong *strategic* competencies as they make decisions about the future. What services are needed in the community? What are the major issues and trends in the external environment that will affect the institution? For example, what are the ethical implications when hospitals open outpatient clinics and offices only in affluent neighborhoods?

The need for *educational* competencies becomes obvious as the board learns about effective trusteeship. Seminars, speakers at meetings, and committee reports all improve a board's information base. For the purposes of this book, trustees should encourage the institution's ethicists to lead an annual conversation on ethical issues as part of their ongoing education.

Analytical competencies allow the board to look at complex issues from numerous perspectives. Opening a suburban office building brings up financial, medical, community, legal, professional, regulatory, and insurance issues. The board must reconcile these numerous perspectives.

Political competencies help the board to develop and reinforce open communication with the numerous constituents who have a stake in its decisions. For example, what if the decision to build a new office building requires the relocation of homes and small businesses? Poor political skills will doom the project very quickly.

Finally, board members need strong *interpersonal skills* to develop into a cohesive group. This does not mean that every decision will be unanimous; rather, it means that different views are allowed to emerge without rancor and division.

In review, these six competencies have been shown to improve board effectiveness. But how do organizations change their internal culture? Skills alone do not lead directly to change. Although they are essential elements in any long-term change strategy, the organization's culture has an effect on internal behavior beyond any single policy decision or edict. Thus, the board needs to practice and reinforce these competencies and understand the ethical implications of their decisions and actions.

Using Board Competencies

Think about how your board learns new ideas, how it moves beyond following established paths. There is rarely time to go beyond a tight board agenda, to question, to discuss, to explore. Thus, consider the memorandum from a hospital chair and CEO in case 2-1.

Case 2-1. The Annual Board Retreat

MEMORANDUM

TO: Board of Trustees

FROM: Chair and CEO

RE: Annual Board Retreat

It is time to plan for the annual board retreat. As usual, the retreat is a daylong, informal seminar on a timely topic important to board functioning. We have all heard about issues regarding privacy and confidentiality of patient information, patient bills of rights, shutdowns of respected medical research centers, threatened government penalties for conflicts of interest, and fears about fraud and abuse audits. Therefore, the planning committee has decided to devote this year's retreat to current issues in medical ethics. The committee hopes this will serve as the beginning of an ongoing ethics program for the board.

This workshop will begin with breakfast and conclude before dinner. We look forward to seeing you at the Regent's Hotel, Conference Room A, on June 16.

Questions for discussion:

1. Has your board conducted such extended discussions?
2. How satisfactory have the processes and outcomes been?
3. What further steps may be needed to strengthen policies and practices relating to ethical issues?

A health care organization's (HCO's) governing body sets the tone for the institution's culture and work climate; it becomes the moral backbone. Indeed, if the board lacks moral authority, there is little likelihood that the system's culture will maintain a strong ethical climate. To set high standards throughout the hospital or health care system, the board must establish the proper ethical climate for its own operations. Changing one's own behavior is a prerequisite for changing the behavior of others. With experience in applying ethical analysis, the board can create a systematic process for integrating ethics into its work.

Once trustees get in the habit of considering ethics as part of their regular responsibilities, they become role models for the institution. The board sends a clear message when it considers ethical conduct to be at the heart of the facility's mission and when it supports open ethical discussions throughout the organization. By creating its own ethical climate of openness and vigorous discussion, the board encourages high standards throughout the organization.

We believe that every health care facility needs a *structured, comprehensive, formalized,* and *documented* ethics program. Because of expanding standards of the JCAHO and greater federal regulations governing research of animal and human subjects, a formal ethics program is a necessity in today's health care environment. A comprehensive program should include an evaluation of the board's own operations and functioning.

In creating an internal board ethics program, the CEO and board chair who wrote the memo in case 2-1 have decided to use the annual retreat as their starting point. By devoting the majority of the time at the retreat discussing biomedical ethics, the board sets an example for others. The goal is to help the board members develop an ethics vocabulary and basic ethical analysis skills so they can integrate ethics into board operations. This will certainly fulfill the educational competency mentioned earlier in the chapter.

The day's agenda might look something like this:

9:00–9:15 a.m.	Welcome and introductions—comments from the CEO and board chair
9:15–9:45 a.m.	Introduction to the vocabulary of medical ethics
9:45–10:45 a.m.	Case discussion
10:45–11:00 a.m.	Break
11:00–Noon	Learning to identify one's own moral filters
Noon–1:30 p.m.	Lunch—point/counterpoint with a bioethicist and a lawyer: "Ethics and Law: Compatibilities and Frictions"
1:30–2:30 p.m.	Review of the case and discussion of alternative conclusions
2:30–3:15 p.m.	General brainstorming about what the board members see as possible components of an internal board ethics program
3:15–3:30 p.m	Break
3:30–4:30 p.m.	Developing action plans and reviewing lessons learned
4:30–4:45 p.m.	Closing remarks

The Vocabulary of Medical Ethics

Let's assume that everyone on the board is an ethical and morally decent individual. That doesn't mean that she or he is able to think through the ethical implications of a situation in a systematic and organized fashion. Being able to do so is the first step toward setting an example for others. If trustees expect to create and sustain high ethical standards, it is imperative for them to analyze ethics issues in a formal, systematic way using the language of ethical analysis.

What basic knowledge is required? A common starting point is an introduction to four ethical principles that guide the conduct of medicine, both in clinical care and biomedical research. They are:

1. Respect for autonomy
2. Nonmalfeasance
3. Beneficence
4. Justice

These principles are familiar to all practicing health care clinicians and researchers and are probably already familiar to many members of a board.

Respect for autonomy has a twofold meaning. First, it requires that we *respect each person's values, perspectives, and capacities; and work to enable others to act as self-determining agents.* The second part of the definition of the principle of respect for persons is just as important, but it is often forgotten or overlooked. It requires that *appropriate protections be provided when individuals have limitations on their autonomous decision making.* This staunch support of self-determination comes out of our political and philosophic traditions that value individual freedom.

The principles of nonmalfeasance and beneficence can be thought of as bookend principles. One of the most ancient ethical norms of medicine, *nonmalfeasance* calls on us *to do no harm and to avoid harm.* A basic tenet of the practice of medicine and the conduct of biomedical research, *beneficence* calls on us *to do, and to promote, good.* Taken together, these two ethical principles help us in the ever-changing evaluation of risks, burdens, and potential benefits of treatment interventions or policy recommendations.

Justice requires us *to ensure fairness,* often through an equitable distribution of benefits and burdens. Although there is much debate about what constitutes a just distribution, fundamentally it means that we should treat persons who are equally situated equally. And when persons are situated unequally, we may have to treat them differently in order to ensure fairness overall.

Although these definitions appear brief and relatively simple to grasp, they are complex in their application. Ordinarily, we speak of these principles as *prima facie,* first on the face of things. That is, a prima facie principle carries a duty that is always to be acted upon unless it is in conflict with a principle that carries an equal or stronger duty. How these ethical principles can come into tension is best seen in the context of a real situation.

Case 2-2. Patients with Deep Pockets

You are a trustee who recently learned the following: It has long been the practice of your nonprofit hospital, as was common throughout the nonprofit hospital industry, to use information from patients' records for hospital fund-raising. When a patient identified as having deep pockets entered the hospital, the Development and Advancement Department got access to that patient's diagnosis to more precisely target fund-raising requests.

Given the privacy and confidentiality concerns that have surfaced in the media—and that have been and are being reviewed in Congress, the federal government, and state legislatures—this practice is being questioned. Therefore, should staff members ask all patients being admitted if they are willing to be approached by hospital fund-raisers?

Questions for discussion:

1. Which of the basic ethical principles does this case raise?
2. In what ways might some or all of these principles be in conflict?
3. How would you weight the various principles and formulate the board's duties?

Some trustees may feel that all four principles play a role in the case and that, at a minimum, the principles of autonomy and non-malfeasance are at stake. Questions arising from this conflict may include:

- How can patients' privacy and confidentiality be protected from inappropriate uses of a medical record?

- How can the hospital ensure that patients are given the opportunity to decide how their private medical information is used and by whom?

- Do development personnel have a legitimate right to private medical information? Does this fund-raising practice contribute to a fair distribution of goods across patients and/or society? If so, in what ways?

- Are individual rights being violated? If so, are such infringements ethically justifiable?

Identifying Moral Filters

In medicine, the basic ethical principles of autonomy, nonmalfeasance, beneficence, and justice are often cited as reasons for doing or not doing something. But if we think about it for a moment, to say that we uphold these principles is little more than platitude. Who doesn't want to treat persons respectfully, supporting and protecting their right to self-determination? Who wants to do harm? We all intend to do good—that is why people choose health careers and why trustees agree to serve on hospital boards. And we all want to be fair and just. So simply knowing how to define these principles is not sufficient to help us begin analyzing ethical issues in systematic ways.

We need to look at ethical theories. One need not view these as dusty, obscure, arcane notions. Quite the contrary. We all use these theories every day when we make decisions about what we ought to do. Ethics can be thought of as the discipline of "oughtness," asking the questions: "What ought I do?" "How ought I act?" "Who ought I be?" Ethical theories resemble our gut responses to the world. We use these analyses daily—when we decide whether to allow another driver to move into our lane, or when we decide whether we're going to spend an extra hour at work or make it home in time to help our children with their homework. These are common ethical decisions. They occur in the same way every day in a hospital: whether to wait to talk to a frail patient about his or her prognosis when it is convenient for us or to reorganize our schedule to allow that conversation to occur after the patient's spouse has arrived. Thinking of ethical theories as moral filters or as subconscious world views helps us understand how we make ethical recommendations and decisions. They are grounded in the ethical ways in which we see the world around us.

The ethical theories or gut ways in which we make moral judgments include the following:

- Consequentialist ethical theories—looking at outcomes
- Duty-based ethical theories—looking at responsibilities
- Virtue-based ethical theories—looking at motives

Consequentialist Ethical Theory

Consequentialist ethical theory states that the way to judge whether an action is right or good is to determine if the consequences of that action will be right or good. We often base our recommendations and decisions on our predictions of consequences. We may feel like driving eighty-five miles per hour in a new sports car, but we don't. We don't because we know that there's a high probability of dire consequences. At the very least, we may get a speeding ticket. At worst, we can do serious harm to others.

But all theories have their weaknesses; here the problem is that predicting future consequences is an imperfect process. Thus, when we are inclined to say that we should or shouldn't do something based on how we think it will turn out, we need to pause and evaluate both our assumptions and predictions.

Duty-Based Ethical Theory

Duty-based ethical theory (also referred to as deontologic ethical theory) says that we should determine if an action is right or good based on whether the person performing the action met his or her duties and obligations. Clinicians are taught ethics from a duty-based perspective. Codes of ethics guide behavior, but it is often difficult to clearly delineate the scope and depth of one's duties and obligations. For example, most persons in health care would agree that the patient ought to come first. But today, with so much medical care being provided within a for-profit setting, the board can be expected to feel a duty not only to the patients served but also to stockholders and to a managed care group's policyholders. In addition, the nonprofit hospital recognizes a duty to the community and to its employees. It is difficult to ascertain just how many persons and entities one has duties and obligations to and how to weigh and balance these effectively.

Virtue-Based Ethical Theory

The most ancient of the three theories, virtue-based ethics, takes a slightly different tack. Rather than make statements about how we should judge an act, it focuses on how we should judge the actor. That is, the way we determine what is right or good is by assessing whether the motives and intentions of the person performing the act were virtuous.

How often have we had a colleague or family member act in a cranky, short-tempered way? Yet we are able to brush it off by saying to ourselves: "Oh, he's just had a bad day. He didn't mean to be nasty to me personally." That is a classic virtue ethics analysis. In much the same way, virtue ethics undergirds much of our judicial system. If you are caught doing something wrong, you are punished. If it is determined that you intended to do something wrong before you did it, you usually get a harsher punishment.

The problem with virtue-based ethics, of course, is that it is impossible to see motives. Although we are more inclined to attribute good and virtuous motives to those we know, like, and trust, the health care system today reduces the prospects for knowing the physicians who work at our hospital. There is little time to establish a personal, trusting relationship. Furthermore, competitive market forces overshadow the health care delivery and research systems in this country and contribute to a serious decrease in the public's trust and goodwill. This reduces the inclination to attribute virtuous motives to anyone.

Attributing motives is made more complex because of the power differentials between providers, the institution, patients, and family members. The patient and family are always going to be at a disadvantage. Patients are patients because they are sick. They and their families are often experiencing pain and suffering and may be in a medical, psychological, or financial crisis. Under such circumstances, persons want desperately to trust the motives of their doctors, other health care providers, hospitals, and health care systems.

On the other hand, the commercialization of medicine turns the patient into a customer and the treatment into something like a commercial transaction. Just using the language of commerce undermines trust. Patients are not customers. Customers imply equals engaged in negotiation about buying and selling a commodity. Patients can never be equals because of the difference in power between patient and clinician.

Trusting the motives of our clinicians or their institutions has indeed become difficult. But building and retaining the trust of patients, families, and the community may be the most important asset a hospital can have. Thus, rather than being some arcane philosophical theory, virtue ethics provides an important perspective on board responsibilities.

Feminist Ethics

There are two additional contemporary ethical theories that have important implications for analyzing the ethical issues of a hospital board. The first, feminist ethics, teaches that the social world has been constructed with gender biases built into the fabric of our communities and institutions. Any categorically stigmatizing bias (such as race, age, ethnicity, or disability) must be eradicated if we are to uphold the principle of justice. Furthermore, feminist ethics takes issue with the traditional ethical theories that suggest ethical decision making should be devoid of emotion and context free. Instead, feminist ethics posits that our emotions serve as guides to what is morally relevant about a situation. The situation's specifics and the relationships of those involved contribute to defining ethically acceptable solutions.

This theoretical perspective has implications for board action. For example, the way the board responds to entrenched power hierarchies will send different kinds of messages throughout an organization. Some power differences among staff members are appropriately grounded in knowledge differentials. Each profession has its own functional knowledge base and competencies. When these are applied in the best traditions of medicine, the patient benefits. But when it comes to moral decision making, there should be a more democratic process to flatten inappropriate power hierarchies. No person or job title has a lock on what is right or good.

According to feminist ethical thought, one way to flatten inappropriate power structures is to move away from the zero-sum game in which one "side" must win at the expense of the other. Instead, through a more open, democratized process of ethical discussion, the board can demonstrate that a consensus-building process is able to produce creative solutions that most people can endorse. This will replace decisions made by fiat and behind closed doors. Such a process may test whether the board really wants a serious ethics program or is only inclined to give lip service to ethics.

Community Values

The other contemporary theory of note is communitarian ethics, which urges the board to consider community values. This notion has important implications for board actions. At a time when diversity and cultural awareness have become organizational buzzwords, open consideration of cultural values and how they affect a specific situation is essential.

Using Moral Filters

The trick to using moral filters is not simply knowing these different ethical perspectives and being able to define them. The key is to apply them to one's own ways of thinking and acting. Just about every action we take has ethical implications. The example of making the judgment not to drive eighty-five miles per hour is a moral decision justified on the basis of a consequentialist analysis. That is, we decide not to drive that fast because we predict the bad consequences will outweigh the good consequences of getting that thrill from driving fast. Our decision represents a moral judgment.

The way in which trustees arrive at their own judgment of whether the case's fund-raising practice is ethically acceptable depends on how each board member weighs ethical principles and applies ethical filters. For example, let us consider the case of patients with deep pockets. We'll take the perspective of a board member who tends toward viewing actions in terms of their potential consequences. She may believe that it is critically important that her small, rural community hospital not miss any opportunity to approach a potential big donor. After all, it is only fair that rich patients who benefit from the excellent care contribute to the community by supporting the hospital so it can provide the same level of excellent care to the community's poor. And she also believes that the hospital's fund-raising staff members are highly discreet with confidential information. One can easily see how this board member might conclude that it is important to continue the practice, even if patients are not informed.

Another board member, however, may come at the problem from a different, duty-based perspective, weigh the principles differently, and reach a different moral judgment. This board member thinks one of the most important duties of any hospital is to keep private patient information confidential and to protect patient information from even the remotest possibility of a breach of confidentiality. Furthermore, this trustee thinks giving patients sufficient information to decide whether they want to share their private information is central to what a trustworthy hospital must do. This board member might agree that there is nothing inherently wrong with the practice of using personal diagnostic information for development purposes but insists that the board require that patients be asked if they are willing to have their information used this way and be provided a means for refusing.

A third board member may come to the same conclusion as the first board member but reach that conclusion through a virtue-based thought process. This board member thinks the practice is fine because it raises funds to help the hospital do its excellent work. But this board member thinks nothing should be mentioned about it in the admission information. First of all, it has been standard industry practice to do it, and no harm has been identified after all these years. And if the hospital were to inform patients now, it might raise suspicions that the hospital was using personal patient information for many reasons, only one of which is raising money. This board member is concerned that sharing such information with patients as they are coming in the door will heighten patient anxiety just at a time when they are already anxious and perhaps in pain.

Thus, it is easy to see how thoughtful trustees can disagree. That is why simply learning the basic ethical principles is not sufficient for board members to set an example. Board members must become skilled in recognizing their own ethical filters and how they weigh the ethical principles and perspectives to justify why things should be done one way or another. Given that the board is responsible for making policy and setting priorities, individual self-awareness and open and vigorous ethical discussions are critically important skills for the board to master. Let's focus on how this happens.

Integrating Ethical Perspectives

Although it is likely that some board members will prefer one or another of the ethical theories already discussed, others will want to integrate these theories into a framework that may be applied whenever a problem arises. A board should develop an approach that everyone can use. Here are some steps to guide such a process.

Step one: Ensure that the board is fully informed of the facts of the situation. The board should understand the relevant information about the patient (or staff member) and family, the organizational issues or health care issues (including facts about diagnosis, treatment, and results), and other pertinent circumstances.

Step two: Identify who is involved and what is at stake for each of them. Explore the claims and views of all parties involved in the situation. The perspectives and concerns of the patient and family members, the health care staff members, the administrators, and others with a legitimate interest in the situation should be understood and respected.

Step three: Define the ethical issues relevant to the situation. In what ways is respect for individual autonomy a part of the matter before the board? Likewise, how are matters of fairness, beneficence, and nonmalfeasance involved here? What motives, responsibilities, outcomes, power differences, and possible biases are relevant to any decision?

Step four: Identify the relevant ethical issues each alternative presents. For example, in what ways would fund-raising choices deal with matters of respecting personal privacy and autonomy? How would they deal with benefits to the community from funds raised? In what ways would each of the alternatives for dealing with a development staff member handle issues of fairness toward the individual and other staff members, risks and consequences for the organization, power differences, community trust, and other relevant ethical principles? Matters of prior commitments, resources required by each option, and other constraints should also be considered in these deliberations.

Weighing the relative importance of the various ethical dimensions of alternative actions is difficult and time consuming. The process may involve differences of opinion among those engaged in it, all of which should be respectfully considered. Many ethical dilemmas do not yield to perfect solutions, so human limitations must be recognized in the search for a conclusion. Likewise, the group should resist pressures to jump to a quick solution and risk overlooking relevant aspects of the problem or the alternative responses.

Doing nothing is, of course, a choice with its own consequences, so the board should recognize and weigh such an option. Intentional delay while the group works toward a solution would be more defensible than merely tabling the matter or rushing to judgment. At some point, however, a choice should be made and presented to others.

Step five: Monitor results and inform the board at a future date of the consequences of its decisions and choices. Coming to a conclusion on a problem may leave some secondary aspects unresolved or be a great relief, especially if the matter has high visibility or major consequences for the organization. Soon thereafter, the board should set aside some time to reflect on the experience and identify lessons it learned that may be applied in future situations of ethical challenges. What worked well in the ways the group dealt with the problem, and what did not? What contributed to making the process go well, and what limited it? What conclusions could the group draw about its work that would assist it in such situations in the future? These reflections will strengthen the board's effectiveness in dealing with future challenges.

In sum, the first three steps establish the basis for board decisions. With the relevant facts, viewpoints, and ethical principles understood, it is now appropriate to identify the alternative decisions or courses of action that may be taken (including possibly doing nothing). For example, in the fund-raising case, the hospital could consider alternatives which:

- Preclude any nonmedical use of patient information
- Require explicit consent from the patient before making any other use of the information, or
- Allow development staff members to use the information for approaching that individual

This process ensures that board members review their choices before taking action. The key principles leading to decisions should be clearly stated along with criteria for monitoring the results of the decision. The time used before making a decision will save numerous problems later on when the wrong action is taken or implemented inappropriately.

Enhancing the Board's Ethical Perspectives

Clearly, mission should drive decision making for the board of trustees. In a *McKinsey Quarterly* article, "Building a Stronger Board," the authors describe a four-step process:

1. Hold a discussion that leads to a definition of the organization, its services, programs, and assets.

2. Disseminate the definition to all committees, key leaders, and relevant employees.

3. Develop procedures to deal with issues as they arise.

4. Report regularly to the government, insurance companies, employees, and others.[4]

So what can your board do to enhance its ethical perspectives? At each board meeting, members should discuss a current ethics issue that has been in the news since the last board meeting. All that is required is to select the newspaper or journal article and include it in the materials that go out to the board ahead of the meeting.

Other suggestions include the following:

• Putting the ethics program director on the board agenda
• Including a summary of ethical issues in the board's background materials
• Having a board member volunteer to attend ethics committee meetings on a regular basis and report back to the board

The next chapter builds on these ideas and provides guidance for creating an ethical culture that supports open dialogue with numerous points of view. The results justify the time and energy needed to explore alternatives in programs and patient care. The identification of these alternatives is important if the hospital or health system is to implement its mission fully and effectively.

References

1. E. A. Johnson, "The Practicing Physician's Role in Hospital Management—An Administrator's View," *Hospital Progress* 50, no. 11 (September 1969): 65.

2. See, for example, the response of the Montana legislature in Senate Bill 342, 6 February 2003, at http://data.opi.state.mt.us/bills/2003/billhtml/SB0342.htm.

3. T. P. Holland, R. A. Ritvo, and A. R. Kovner, *Improving Board Effectiveness: Practical Lessons for Health Care Organizations* (Chicago: American Hospital Publishing, 1997). See also T. P. Holland, "Board Accountability: Lessons from the Field," *Nonprofit Management and Leadership* 12, no. 4 (Summer 2002): 409–28.

4. R. F. Felton, A. Hudnut, and V. Witt, "Building a Stronger Board," *McKinsey Quarterly* 2 (1995): 162–75.

3

Creating the Ethical Organization

A T ITS CORE, governance is using ethics to address the major issues an organization faces. Although the provision of health care is certainly an ethically worthy endeavor in general, the board has further specific responsibilities, including deciding *how* the organization will carry out the provision of health care, deal with competing interests, and formulate the goals it will pursue.

As Paul B. Hofmann points out in *Trustee* magazine:

> Trustees are guardians of the hospital's integrity. They have the obligation and perhaps the burden of serving as the organization's conscience. Most trustees do not seek this particular role and may not like to be so designated, but they *are* the moral agents of their institutions. One very tangible way to demonstrate a genuine commitment to this dimension of hospital governance is through the systematic development and monitoring of appropriate policies that reflect an ethical sensitivity to the needs of patients, families, and health care professionals.[1]

Board members should not make arrogant pronouncements on the ethical components of issues they face, but they *should* develop and exercise such expertise in ways that complement their skills in finances and fund-raising, strategic planning, evaluation, and public diplomacy. Trustees should be sensitive to the ethical issues facing the organization and capable of making a reflective analysis of those issues.

This is not to say that differences of emphasis and insight will never arise in such discussions. Diverse perspectives are important for thorough work on such difficult matters, but trustees should draw together into a cohesive group whose members share a willingness to establish and sustain the ethical character of the organization for which they have taken responsibility. Trustees should be trustworthy, willing to take risks, and committed to strengthening the quality of their work on behalf of the organization and the community.

The Iowa Hospital Association's "Guidelines for Trustee Self-Assessment" stresses the crucial role of the hospital governing board: to ensure that the hospital provides high-quality, affordable care that meets community and area needs.[2] In its guidelines, the association offers the following pathways to meeting the following needs:

- "Establishing a philosophy and mission statement and approving goals, objectives, and policies with a system for monitoring their implementation"
- "Ensuring adequacy of funding both for current operations and future needs"
- "Planning for the future successful operation of the hospital"
- "Maintaining [a] public relations program which ensures [that the] community's voice is heard on the board, [and] that hospital policy and operations are understood by the citizens, community leaders and local government"
- "Ensuring that the hospital is effectively managed through recruitment, selection and retention of the best possible CEO"
- "Accountability for [the] quality [of] care provided"
- "Ensuring the effective functioning of the board"

The guidelines also state: "Developing strategies to influence today's governing board also recognizes the need to influence the broader political and economic environment in which the hospital operates."

Turning Ideas into Action

Effective governance establishes an organization's culture and behavior as well as the ethical climate for the hospital's internal community. High-quality health care delivery calls for a governance process to develop, maintain, and reward a culture that continually brings out the best in the organization's personnel. All employees and trustees must understand the importance of moral choices, how previous decisions become the starting point for contemporary ones, and how all members can increase self-awareness about their own moral filters. The following letter from the daughter of a patient in ICU to her sister illustrates how these filters work—or do not.

Case 3-1. Edith's Guilt

Dear Susan,

How are you and Martin? Please tell him how much I appreciated your being here these past nine weeks with Dad and me. Now that Dad's funeral is over, I keep wondering what we could have done differently. As I look back over the horrible weeks with Dad in the ICU, I know we did everything we could to communicate Dad's wishes. Why didn't anyone listen to us? We knew what Dad wanted. All that seemed to matter was his separate organ systems. Didn't you get so tired of listening to them tell us, "Your father's liver functions are stable today," when he just lay there, motionless. Or: "Your father's breathing a little stronger today." What difference did it make, when he was never going to get off that terrible machine and they all knew it? We kept telling them he didn't want to live like that. The doctors and nurses simply knew him by his different parts. I feel so guilty that we failed him. Do you?

Love,

Edith

Questions for discussion:

1. Who (if anyone) failed Edith, Susan, and their father?
2. What are the ethical issues at stake in this situation?
3. In what ways could the staff members have addressed Edith's concerns more effectively?
4. What organizational policies may be needed to support such actions?

There are many social and medical taboos and rituals surrounding death. All things being equal, nobody wants to die or to be dying. No doubt, fear of death and our valiant struggles to avoid it are genetically programmed. It would be difficult to ensure the survival of the species if it were easy to let go. We expect health care providers to be vigorous in their efforts to save our life, to cure our diseases. When it gets easy for clinicians to withhold or withdraw life-extending technologies, such as antibiotics, respirators, and dialysis machines, we should suspect burnout and take corrective measures. At the bedrock of medical ethics is this principle: "When in doubt, err on the side of life."

However, not every technologically possible effort should be made to stand in the way of death—only every *appropriate* effort. What is an appropriate effort? And what processes are in place to assist persons (such as clinicians, risk managers, lawyers, and administrators) who make these gut-wrenching and emotionally exhausting determinations? Often intellectually challenging, ethically complicated, and legally precarious, such decisions cause much of the distress felt in today's hospitals. That is why the issues surrounding death and dying—and especially the decisions to withhold or withdraw treatment—are critical for trustees to understand. Only then can they develop clear policies and procedures for the staff members in their facility.

Susan and Edith provided care for their father at the end of his life, and as the letter shows, there is a residue of sadness and guilt. How could this terminal care have been provided differently? How could the hospital and its clinicians have contributed to making his death easier for the patient and the family?

Beginning at the level of the individual clinician, there should have been a meeting to discuss goals for the patient's plan of care. Such a discussion would include the two sisters, the patient's private attending physician, the intensive care unit (ICU) attending physician(s), nurses, the social worker or case manager assigned to the patient, and, if appropriate, hospital clergy. If that meeting did not produce a consensus on a treatment plan, at least one more meeting could have been held with the hospital's clinical ethicist or the hospital's ethics committee. Then the sisters could have made clear their understanding of their father's wishes. The fact that their father did not write down his wishes in an advance directive document, such as a living will, or by assigning a durable power of attorney for health care need not be an insurmountable problem medically, ethically, or legally.

The Legal Department

The legal department can assist in establishing an ethical climate in the hospital. By serving as an ex officio member on the hospital's ethics committee, an attorney can provide legal opinions about the reasonable boundaries for making clinical and ethical recommendations. This allows the committee to better define ethically permissible options for the case's decision makers—the professionals caring for the patient and the patient or the patient's surrogates. Usually, this is a collaborative and collegial process in which the parties involved can agree that the focus must be to act in the patient's best interest.

When the law is ambiguous or silent, sound advice to the clinicians and to the ethics committee is to do what is best for the patient. Health care professionals need to know that the legal counsel will support and defend actions based on ethical analysis.

Many lawyers tend to take a more traditional view, giving their clinicians and hospital administrators conservative advice, essentially telling them to practice defensive medicine. We believe that practicing defensive medicine comes at the expense of thoughtful involvement of the patient and family and results in suboptimal medicine. And practicing suboptimal medicine is the surest road to lawsuits that the hospital can be expected to lose.

Malpractice Lawsuits

No legal advice, good or bad, can prevent a lawsuit. That is one of the great accomplishments of our democratic society and our Constitution. Anybody can file a lawsuit. The important issue is whether a suit has merit. Because most suits are brought against physicians, trustees need to have a basic understanding of this process.

Before the mid-1950s, lawsuits against doctors were mostly brought on the grounds of a battery claim. If there was fraud or misrepresentation involved in obtaining a patient's consent to surgery, the consent was not effective and the surgery would therefore be a battery. More recently, malpractice suits are often grounded in negligence theory. Negligence theory imports the notion of standards. That is, if a doctor failed to meet the community medical practice standard of care for, say, the disclosure of common risks of a particular childhood vaccine, then the physician could be held accountable for negligence if injury occurred. The standards of conduct require that the physician have the knowledge and skills of a member of that professional group in good standing in the same or similar communities. The standard of care is care that the reasonable professional would provide.

Excessive fear of lawsuits leads physicians to make bad medical decisions and communicate poorly with patients and families. Our best advice to doctors and nurses is to be the best doctors and nurses they can be. We believe, further, that doing so is the ethical ideal in addition to being the best legal protection. A comprehensive, hospitalwide ethics program, beyond just an ad hoc panel with specific decisions, can also provide legal protection.

Ethical and legal issues tend to bump up against each other and cause friction. If clinicians become too fearful of negligence or wrongful death suits, the quality of medical care is reduced but not the number of suits brought against hospitals and doctors. If anything, we believe that such fears may put the institution at greater risk. Instead, collaborative working relationships between the legal and risk management departments will result in proper ethical discussion, deliberation, and debate. But that doesn't mean that everything is always smooth sailing.

An important role for the board is to understand and respond to the power of the medical establishment inherent in health care organizations. Some of these physicians are appropriately grounded in knowledge and skill differentials. Each profession has its functional knowledge base and competencies. When these are applied in the best traditions of medicine and health care, the patient benefits.

But when it comes to moral decision making, there should be a more democratic process. Given how entrenched medical hierarchies are, this is a tall order. But it is a necessary one if we are ever really to have a responsible delivery system. Part of this process is to move away from the primacy of the zero-sum game. There are integrative solutions that trustees must work to find within clear ethical guidelines.

Because laws, like ethical norms, are open to interpretation, persons of good judgment can disagree. Thus, it is important to create an institutional climate that acknowledges disagreement is useful. "It is good to disagree. Let us disagree agreeably." The point is that task-focused, thoughtful, substantive, and sophisticated argument leads to finding the best answer to a particular problem at a particular point in time. It also allows participants to develop a sense of respect for multiple perspectives. Trustees must learn to appreciate that ethical analysis is a tough process requiring time and thoughtful communication. No matter how thoroughly considered an ethically complex issue may be, there might never be an unequivocally "right answer." Even if there were at one moment, circumstances change (a patient's prognosis, an organizational situation, or a regulatory change). Then the analysis needs to be repeated.

Widening the Focus

Words have real and symbolic meaning. The language of health care changes with each generation. Examine the terms in figure 3-1 and see how today's rhetoric differs from that used a generation ago.

Figure 3-1. The Changing Rhetoric of Health Care

The word . . .	emphasizes . . .	and defines health care as . . .
Patient	"Cared for by providers"	Service
Client	"Needs dominate process"	Service
Consumer	"Staff members meet their needs"	Product
Customer	"Staff roles are defined by what the customer wants or needs"	Product

These shifts represent real and symbolic change in health care delivery and its major components.

How we refer to users of the health care system does make a difference. In fact, calling them *customers* rather than *patients* highlights the activist notion of the term. Providers are seeing fewer compliant patients who passively follow instructions and more customers searching for second opinions and alternative treatment approaches.

These changes have profound implications for all health care providers, requiring a broader perspective than we had a few decades ago. Taking a systems approach to integrating ethics throughout the organization can mitigate some of the friction these changes might cause. This is where the ethicist can play an important role.

Ethicists exist to ask challenging questions. Of course, they can assist in identifying ethically acceptable boundaries, but once those boundaries are set, an ethicist's opinion is only the ethicist's opinion. Although ethicists become useful and widely sought out because their opinions are reasonable and sound (even sometimes wise!), it is critical to remember that persons of good judgment often disagree. What ethicists do best, unlike good attorneys, risk managers, or successful compliance programs, is produce more questions than answers. So when the ethicist illuminates the gray zones, it is often in direct opposition to what attorneys and risk managers want to have happen and what is taught by most compliance programs.

Often, one of the members of the ethics committee is from risk management and another is an institutional lawyer serving as either a regular or an ex officio committee member. The institution's risk managers and legal counsel should be well trained in ethics and not inclined to foster fearful, punitive behavior, which creates conflict and impedes open conversation.

For some reason there is an assumption that people sue hospitals and physicians more for actions *not* taken than for actions they *do* take. But clinicians and institutions are sued both for doing things and for not doing things. There have been well-publicized suits over issues related to withholding or withdrawing life-sustaining measures, and such suits have been brought and won. There is little rhyme or reason for the outcome of any particular set of circumstances. The fact is that cases are most often grounded in breakdowns in communication and trust.

Thus, good medicine dictates that medical/moral decisions—and most medical decisions have a moral component to them—must be grounded in good clinical practice, fair and open consideration of the medical and ethical factors of a case, and open communication with patients and family members. Decisions should be decided on the basis of the basic medical/ethical principle of acting in the best interest of the patient. This upholds the principle of beneficence.

Should hospitals allow the risk manager and the attorney to control these decisions because they have some preconceived notions about what actions will put the institution at a lower risk of being sued? No. An atmosphere that fosters high ethical standards takes into account all relevant perspectives, including legal and risk management, through a sound process of reflective ethical analysis. Trustees should be sure that such discussions include perspectives from the ethics committee, the hospital's administrative structure, clinicians, and representatives of patients and families as appropriate. Such discussions require a thoughtful processing of how the medical, ethical, and psychosocial aspects of the case are influenced by the systematic application of the ethical principles and theories.

A key function of the board is to make certain that the hospital is a safe place in which to have vigorous ethical disagreements.[3] One critical way in which this safe environment is created is to reduce the stranglehold that the risk management and legal departments have on clinician decision making. Yes, it is true that the number of lawsuits against physicians, hospitals, and health care organizations has risen markedly over the past forty years. Yes, it is also true that groups such as Public Citizen and the Florida Department of Insurance provide the public with information about who has been sued and the monetary awards. But it is just as true that many legitimate claims are never filed. Furthermore, there is a growing sense that many lawsuits filed against physicians are the result of mismanaging the emotional aspects of medical care. That is, it may not be the actual outcome that determines whether a patient decides to sue, but rather the perceived quality of the relationship, trust, and communication between the patient and the physician that drive such lawsuits. And although the admonition to drive defensively may be a proper approach when behind the wheel of a car, it can be toxic in the health care arena. "Practice forthrightly and courageously" may be better advice, but advice not often given by hospital risk managers or attorneys. The board of trustees bears the ultimate responsibility for the culture of medical care in the institution.

When risk managers and hospital attorneys cooperate and are mutually supportive, they are more likely to give the advice to practice forthrightly and courageously. It helps to integrate legal counsel into the ethics process, without allowing legal opinion to substitute for moral values and ethical judgment. This demands that legal counsel never be permitted to trump the process of rigorous ethical analysis. This also demands courage on the part of the administration and the board. When ethical consensus has been reached through a solid and deliberative process, the legal and risk management components of the institution should stand by the decision, even defending it in court.

The goal of a health care organization must never be to "just not get sued." This should always be a by-product of providing excellent health care. Nowhere is this a more important value to uphold than in end-of-life cases. Whether in the surgical ICU, the geriatric unit, or the neonatal unit, making sound decisions requires difficult conversations. The ability to have such conversations is strengthened or weakened in great measure by the moral environment that has been created. That moral environment is greatly affected by the degree to which internal legal counsel and risk managers accept the need to make the most ethically justified decision, not just the safest.

Implications for the Board

Creating a climate in which it is safe to challenge each other on moral matters requires the organizational mission, structures, and leadership to foster ethical practices. Although necessary, it is not sufficient for the board to learn to do that alone. Clear signals must be sent throughout the institution that vigorous moral discourse is not only valued but also expected. One of the most important signals, when a physician is alleged to have engaged in poor behavior, is the institution's quickly and firmly addressing it, even if the doctor is one of its biggest revenue-producing physicians. Everyone needs to know that the system within which they work is fair and just. Furthermore, protections must be in place to ensure that there is never any intimidation or reprisals against those who bring an ethical concern to light. Only by being evenhanded and protecting the weakest can an institution foster an environment of integrity and openness. Such qualities nourish high ethical standards and professionalism.

Ethical Actions

As Michael Daigneault writes in *Board Member,* the following keys to successful ethical practice will assist trustees:

- Ethics is job one. Trustees create and sustain the values, ethics, and financial integrity of an organization.
- "Nonprofit" means a commitment to the public good and stewardship. Trust is essential to the special relationship nonprofits have with the communities that sustain them.
- Good things happen when ethics is a priority. Benefits include building and sustaining a positive reputation within the communities in which an organization operates as well as recruiting and retaining top-quality staff members and volunteers.
- A focus on ethics improves the organization's integrity. People are willing to donate time and money to organizations they trust.[4]

Finally, having an explicit policy on ethics and scheduling regular discussions of the ethical issues faced by the board and organization have been documented as key practices of highly effective boards.[5] Guidelines for developing such policies and practices may be found in G. E. Kobb's book *Developing an Ethics Program,*[6] and a reflective discussion of the components of board responsibilities in this area may be found in D. H. Smith's book *Entrusted: The Moral Responsibilities of Trusteeship.*[7]

Bylaws and Policies

Attention to ethics in bylaws and institutional policies define the values of the organization and provide a code of conduct for the board and staff. Although a policy by itself cannot prevent wrongdoing, it conveys a strong message both internally and externally about the organization's values and commitments.

The board's commitment to ethical behavior should begin with recognition of this basic responsibility in the organization's bylaws. Bylaws set forth the organization's basic purpose, structure, and governance procedures. Along with statements of the mission and purpose of the organization, duties of its trustees and officers, meetings, records, and other foundational matters, the bylaws should include explicit principles and expectations of ethical behavior the organization pledges to follow in all its work, as well as specific rules regarding how the board will deal with such matters as conflicts of interest.

Officers and trustees have a fiduciary relationship to the organization, meaning they must always act in the best interests of the organization, not of themselves. A committee on ethics may be appointed to develop or refine such statements, prepare more detailed guidelines fitting the organization's circumstances, and ensure the board's understanding and compliance with them. See figure 3-2 for an example of one organization's statement on ethics.

The next chapter focuses on applying these principles in daily practice. Keep in mind the importance of the hospital's mission. It is more than a motto; it should be the model for action. An institution must have systems to protect patients and implement its fiduciary role in the community.

The institution must also have appropriate mechanisms to react when things go awry. Things do indeed go wrong; human beings err. If the error falls in the category of valid intent or faulty action, one set of reactions is warranted. If the intent was malicious (fraud, hiding a mistake, or impairment), alternative approaches would be in order. Most health care professionals and staff members are dedicated to their job, their patients, and their community. The board's role therefore is to ensure that the organization's culture, policies, and internal environment are conducive to employees' doing their

Figure 3-2.   Ethics Policy of Northside Health Care Network

We as the trustees of Northside Health Care Network are dedicated to carrying out the mission of this organization. Toward that end, the staff members and we will:

1. Recognize that the major function of Northside Health Care Network at all times is to serve the best interests of our constituencies.

2. Accept as a personal duty the responsibility to keep current on emerging issues and to conduct ourselves with professional competence, fairness, impartiality, efficiency, and effectiveness.

3. Respect the structure and responsibilities of the board and staff; share information, facts, and principles guiding policy decisions; and uphold policies adopted by this board.

4. Keep the community informed about issues facing the organization and the actions of this board.

5. Conduct our duties with positive leadership exemplified by open communication, creativity, dedication, compassion, and accountability.

6. Exercise our authority responsibly to carry forth the mission of the organization.

7. Serve with respect, concern, courtesy, and responsiveness on carrying out our responsibilities.

8. Demonstrate the highest standards of personal integrity, truthfulness, honesty, and fortitude in all our activities in order to inspire confidence and trust in our actions.

9. Avoid any interest or activity that is in conflict with the conduct of our duties.

10. Respect and protect privileged information to which we have access in the course of our duties.

11. Strive for personal professional excellence and encourage the professional development of others.

best work and demonstrating accountability. That is how an institution fulfills its mission.

References

1. P. B. Hofmann, "Upholding Patient Rights through Ethical Policy-Making," *Trustee* 38, no. 4 (April 1985): 16.
2. Committee on Governing Boards of the Iowa Hospital Association, "Guidelines for Trustee Self-Assessment: Evaluation of Hospital Governing Board Performance" [undated material], pp. 3–4.

3. R. E. Bulger and S. J. Reiser, eds., *Integrity in Health Care Institutions: Humane Environments for Teaching, Inquiry, and Healing* (Iowa City, Iowa: University of Iowa Press, 1990).
4. M. Daigneault, "Board Checklist: Make Ethics a Leadership Priority," *Board Member* 10, no. 10 (2001): 5.
5. T. P. Holland, "Board Accountability: Lessons from the Field," *Nonprofit Management and Leaders* 12, no. 4 (2002): 409–28.
6. G. E. Kobb, *Developing an Ethics Program* (Washington, D.C.: Board Source, 1999).
7. D. H. Smith, *Entrusted: The Moral Responsibilities of Trusteeship* (Bloomington, Ind.: Indiana University Press, 1995).

4

Implementing the Hospital's Mission

PERHAPS the best place to start improving hospital ethics is with your institution's mission statement. Often relegated to the articles of incorporation on file in the secretary of state's archives, the mission statement provides the rationale for the facility's existence. Every trustee, director, administrative officer, provider, and staff member should be familiar with this statement. Indeed, it should be reviewed and updated periodically.

Effective strategic planning begins with the institutional mission. Mission statements do not tell us what to do in the short term; instead, they define a sense of direction, core principles, and organizational values that guide and shape all plans for the future.

To satisfy the corporate ethic, the connection of action to mission must be clear. All programs, services, and decisions should be evaluated for how they contribute to the organizational mission. If the mission is in the nonprofit sector, there may be a different set of values than in proprietary institutions. In both cases, however, personnel, structures, finances, investments, procedures, and assessment processes must be in alignment. Adherence to the mission statement may show itself in disagreements during board meetings. If there are no disagreements, one might wonder how committed the system is to implementing these values because such decisions are not simple and require conversations about means and ends, ethical concerns, public policy, and patient needs. There are no clear, uniform results. If there were, all hospitals would be identical.

Board members must have a passing knowledge of clinical procedures in order to understand the implications of proposals and decisions on the hospital's mission. Conversely, do clinical decision makers need a passing knowledge of public policy and legal issues? Some assert they should not let these external constraints enter their relationship with the patient. Others argue that it is a disservice to a patient if the provider does not give full information about the procedure, financial implications, and other factors related to the patient's entire case. How a board resolves these issues defines its ethical posture and establishes the ethical culture for the organization.

In many religious institutions, the ultimate authority resides in the religious organizational structure. Board members are appointed or elected through the boards of officers. For many Christian facilities, the overriding governing principle is to "glorify Christ in all we do." This higher calling augments the IRS category of a 501(c)(3) organization. Without becoming a proselytizing mission, the staff members in such facilities help patients and clients cope with the physical, emotional, and spiritual dimensions of their illness. At some level, they believe that the healing process is helped when spiritual energy augments the body's own processes and the efforts of the health care staff members.

These values and ethical expectations for service do not reduce the responsibility of the board and CEO to make the difficult economic and financial decisions. They must strive to be good stewards of the community's health and institutional resources. Remember community-focused ethics? It sometimes makes it difficult to reconcile the conflicting values of meeting a documented need and operating efficiently.

Promoting Civility

As a complement to the formal organizational mission, we believe many systems could benefit from statements about respect and civility among employees. How will personnel work together? Service and civility can be stressed in an employee handbook, but the best incentive for employees comes from the performance and expectations of top leaders. When the president strolls through the emergency room checking inventory, that sends a message of control. If the president is there to gain an understanding of the stress on Saturday nights, the staff members learn that respect and information are values of the top leaders. These actions reinforce how the system treats its members, its clients, and the community.

An example of how mission, religious values, and ethical considerations enter the governance process can be found in the decision by a major urban medical center in Alabama to close a failing proprietary health care facility. Rather than abruptly "dump" 225 patients into the community for care, this board decided it was worth the short-term cost to phase down services at the center so other facilities would have time to adapt. This process took several months and gave the community time to adjust. In this case the values of service and ethical principles were more important than the bottom line. The CEO summarized the central issue before the board: "How do we accomplish this without reducing service? Of course, economics are relevant, but they must be tempered by our concern for patients, medical and support staff, and the community. It has to be more than dollars or economics; it must be just."

As hospitals and their boards face mounting pressures from the increasing number of uninsured, decreasing levels of reimbursement, and higher demand for costly care, decisions about how to balance these pressures become more difficult. The following case study and those that follow exemplify these pressures.

Case 4-1. Absorbing Large Costs

A citizen from New Zealand with a long history of chronic obstructive pulmonary disease, diabetes, high blood pressure, and cardiac rhythm disturbances decides to tour Alaska alone. After leaving the Los Angeles airport, she requires a gurney and oxygen because she is so fatigued. She requests to continue to Alaska. Within twenty-four hours after landing in Alaska, she is hospitalized and requires the support of a ventilator. After multiple unsuccessful attempts to wean her off the ventilator, the option of returning her to New Zealand is pursued. She has no financial resources and no insurance. The New Zealand consulate is contacted, and its response is, "We are not responsible financially or otherwise for a private citizen abroad." This individual is consuming resources at the rate of $3,000 per day, and there does not appear to be an obvious solution.

Questions for discussion:

1. How should this be handled?
2. What ethical principles are at stake in this situation?
3. How could the board of this health care organization establish policies to guide staff decisions in such situations?
4. In what ways should those policies be grounded in the organization's mission statement?
5. How well is your board prepared to guide decisions in such situations? Does it need further work in this area?

Trusting a Facility

Trust is one of the most important assets of a health and medical care delivery system. It is the cornerstone of the patient-physician relationship and the foundation of a hospital's reputation. The importance of trustworthiness to medical ethics is evident in the emphasis placed on physician integrity since the writing of the Hippocratic oath. The contemporary American health care system requires trust by the patient and patient's family in others besides the primary physician.

Unfortunately, the current situation is that patients and families must rely on the good intentions of institutions in which the public has generally little trust: commercial insurance companies, government programs, health maintenance organizations, and the large, multitiered institutions where medical care is delivered. Certainly, this is a far cry from the world of Marcus Welby, a physician depicted twenty-five years ago in a nationally popular television series. Dr. Welby practiced in a private office, admitting and discharging patients from a small community hospital where patients trusted those to whom they went for care. In many areas, health care delivery bears no resemblance today to the way care was delivered only two or three decades ago.

Added to these outdated impressions is a general lack of understanding by patients of how hospitals and health systems operate.

The old model depicted hospital inpatients who depended on their physicians and nurses to take care of them. But today the hospital and its environment have become more complicated; now numerous specialists see patients briefly, rendering important opinions but often not participating in the patient's care beyond the hospital stay. These realities of hospital care today are little appreciated by the average patient. Instead, when a member of the public enters a hospital as a patient or as a friend or family member of a patient, that individual tends to trust the institution. The assumption is that the clinicians providing care and the general ethos of the institution are devoted to the well-being of the patient. Generally this is true but not always.

Trust of a hospital, a hospital system, and its clinicians is based on patient/family, professional, and community evaluation of the level of competence and care provided. One of the more important ways to demonstrate competence and a caring attitude is to protect patient privacy and confidentiality.

Maintaining Privacy and Confidentiality

Privacy and confidentiality are distinct concepts. *Privacy* refers to an individual's moral and legal right to control access to matters related to one's private life. Most often, this is considered within the context of medical information, but actually the scope is broader and includes control over zones of intimacy, body products, personal documents, and intimate relationships. *Confidentiality* refers to the control of access to personal information or other private matters after this information or material (such as blood) has been provided to someone else, such as a physician or a laboratory. The belief that providers ought to protect personal information and materials has a long history. Although no one today suggests that patient confidentiality should not be protected, some believe that in actual practice confidentiality often has limits because there are so many people who have a legitimate reason to review personal patient data. Case 4-2 illustrates an alleged breach of privacy and confidentiality.

Case 4-2. Jumping to Conclusions

August 12, 2004

Mr. Arnold T. Smith
President
Community General Hospital
648 Main Street
Smalltownsville, Iowa

Dear Mr. Smith,

This letter summarizes our telephone conversation earlier today. On top of the terrible pain I feel as a result of the death of Don, my beloved husband of forty-six years, I am extremely upset with the hospital. Not only is my husband dead, but because of your hospital's total disregard for our privacy, his good name has been destroyed—and destroyed by a lie.

Fifteen years ago, my husband was in an automobile accident. He was pretty banged up, with broken bones and internal bleeding. During surgery they gave him several units of blood. Gratefully, he recovered fully—or so we thought. Now it appears that he became infected with the hepatitis C virus. Because of the hepatitis, my husband died of cirrhosis of the liver.

We live in a small community where many people think drinking alcohol is a sin. That is why we only had an occasional drink when we were home. Now, because nurses and doctors at your hospital gossiped to their friends or family, the whole town knows. My neighbors are still talking about it. Rather than telling me how sorry they are that Don is gone, they give me lectures on the evils of alcohol. Some of our oldest and, I thought, dearest friends are avoiding me, just when I need their support.

Mr. Smith, my husband was a wonderful man. He was loved and respected in this community and now, because the hospital staff didn't keep the information regarding his death private, his good name has been ruined. People who don't know him think he was some kind of lush. I'm hurt and angry. What's happened to Don's reputation and to me just is not right. Aren't hospitals supposed to keep personal information confidential? You say that's what you will do. But you did not. I'm never going to be able to trust anyone at your hospital. I think the staff should be punished for ruining my husband's reputation. I don't know what can be done, but something needs to be. Please let me know when you have taken action.

Sincerely,

Mrs. Donald Ritter

Questions for discussion:

1. How should Mr. Smith respond to Mrs. Ritter's letter?
2. What ethical principles are at stake in this situation?
3. What policies should the board of this hospital put in place to guide handling such situations in the future?

In the case of Mr. and Mrs. Ritter, there are numerous ways in which the alleged breach of confidentiality could have occurred. The worst possibility is that physicians, nurses, or others with legitimate access to Mr. Ritter's private medical information were gossiping; that could explain how the information about his diagnosis leaked out of the hospital. If this were the case, the gossip might have transpired outside the hospital. In any case, such gossip should never occur. Worse yet, a staff member could have discussed Mr. Ritter's case directly with another patient or visitor. Another inexcusable cause for breaches of confidentiality is sloppiness. The patient's chart might have been left in view of another patient or visitor, who then breached Mr. Ritter's privacy by looking at the information. Or maybe it was just a community rumor not involving the hospital at all.

Although this matter will probably be directed to the legal and risk management departments, it requires a response. Whether such a letter eventually reaches the board or a trustee committee, hospitals must have policies in place to review such allegations. The board needs to be informed, perhaps through an annual summary or risk management report. Certainly, the board and CEO cannot be involved in every patient complaint, but this one is a particularly egregious allegation. Protecting patient privacy and confidentiality is central to the ethical conduct of a hospital. As Mrs. Ritter stated, it can result in a loss of trust in the hospital.

These possibilities for breach of confidentiality constitute unprofessional behavior and are avoidable. It is quite possible that the breach was not by someone gossiping or being careless with patient records but as a result of the architectural aspects of hospital life or by virtue of the very ways in which hospital medicine is performed.

Hospital architecture tends to encourage breaches of confidentiality. Nurses, physicians, and other delivery personnel use nursing stations to exchange information to keep abreast of patient status; these are usually open to view and within easy earshot of others. Nursing stations are close to patient rooms and designed for easy flow of doctors and nurses; as such, ambulatory patients and visitors walk by them. Although nurses and physicians try to keep their voices down and conversations to a minimum, others can overhear information about patients.

As problematic as the architecture of patient floors is the long-standing custom of medical rounds. In any hospital where there are interns or residents, medical rounds ensure that all the medical staff members are regularly briefed on each patient. Rounds are a core tradition of medical education. During rounds, the attending physician assembles the health care team. Once gathered, the team goes from bed to bed, discussing details of each patient's case. This can include a review of the patient's medical history, diagnosis, laboratory findings, and organ-system status. The discussion includes (or should include) a review of the goals and plan for care, prognostic considerations, and pertinent psychosocial and ethical issues.

This daily process for updating the team on the patient's status and for teaching young doctors is a necessary component of good patient care. Where these discussions occur, patient privacy and confidentiality are difficult to maintain. Often, rounds begin outside the patient's room and can easily be overheard. From outside the door, the group moves to the bedside. When patients have roommates, others can easily overhear the discussions held with health professionals.

In the ICUs, the situation is usually even less private. Because of the unstable and critical status of most ICU patients, it is important that nursing staff members easily see and hear patients and their monitors. The implication for information exchange on rounds is obvious. Others in the ICU may be able to hear what is being reported about other patients.

In the case of Mrs. Ritter, let us try to put the best spin on the problem. Let us assume that one of the Ritters' neighbors was visiting another patient and overheard the report on Mr. Ritter. The visitor either didn't hear the part about the transfusion-transmitted hepatitis C or didn't appreciate the significance of the information and only picked up on the diagnosis of cirrhosis of the liver. Because a common cause of cirrhosis is alcohol abuse, this visitor jumped to the incorrect conclusion that the cirrhosis resulted from alcohol abuse. Although neighborly kindness would dictate that private information accidentally overheard not be spread, this visitor is not governed by any of the professional codes requiring protection of privacy and confidentiality that guide health care professionals. The neighbor is less constrained to keep the information private. Even if this last scenario accounts for how the breach took place, thus holding the medical team blameless, a breach of privacy and confidentiality has occurred and damage has been done.

The Board's Role

The board cannot contribute to protecting against such breaches if it has no idea such a case has occurred. Thus, it is important that board members regularly hear about cases that might reduce community trust in the hospital. One way to ensure the board learns about cases such as the Ritters' is to add a privacy and confidentiality section to the materials sent to board members ahead of regular meetings. The borad's discussion of how such a case can be prevented in the future can help the institution develop adaptive procedures. These may be recommended by the CEO or trustees.

How would board members learn about the impact of architectural features on the practice of medicine? Board members need to spend time in the hospital. For example, as part of board member orientation, rather than just being walked through the building(s), trustees might be encouraged to attend ICU rounds. There might be a seat on the hospital's ethics committee for a board member. Whatever avenue is selected to help a board member learn about the workings of the hospital, it may be one of the most important links the board can make with patients and staff members. And such experiences add a level of credibility otherwise impossible to achieve and will help the board demonstrate substance, not produce a show merely for appearance's sake. The difference is readily identifiable.

In some facilities, the board and staff members often deal with sensitive information about patients, one another, donors, volunteers, and others. They are often exposed to confidential information critical to the well-being of the organization. This makes policies about confidential information important to the organization's credibility and reputation. See figure 4-1 for an example of a policy on confidentiality.

Living Wills

We have become enamored with, and hamstrung by, legalistic thinking, not the least of which is exemplified by the deification of documentation. In our attempts to halt excessive paternalism and to ensure that medical care remains consistent with a patient's wishes and preferences, we have become too dependent on written documentation to ensure that a patient's wishes and preferences are followed. Too often, we substitute a legally narrow maxim—"If it isn't written down, it doesn't exist"—for good medical practice about how to care for dying patients. Certainly, having a living will or a signed durable power for health care, which designates a family member or friend to speak for the patient when necessary, assists in providing good medical care.

But living wills are not always assistive. Sometimes these documents are written in confusing, contradictory ways; sometimes they appear to make requests that are inconsistent with sound medical judgment. Long before we had advance directives, physicians made good medical decisions. Historically, those decisions were made without much knowledgeable input from the patient; but often there was important participation of patient surrogates. And many good medical decisions are still made that way, even with minimal patient involvement. Today, in the United States and in a growing number of countries around the world, patients are viewed as the primary decision makers in their own care. Thus, whenever possible, physicians and nurses should be guided directly by patient wishes.

Today we have a prior standard to apply whenever possible: that patients should make their own decisions to the greatest degree possible. This standard is grounded in the principle of respect for persons, or the autonomy principle, and in legal terms is known as the standard of their own judgment. That means that a patient's wishes

Figure 4-1. Confidentiality Policy of Northside Health Care Network

It is the policy of Northside Health Care Network that its trustees and staff may not disclose, divulge, or make accessible confidential information belonging to or obtained through their affiliation with this organization to any person, including relatives, friends, and business and professional associates, other than to persons who have a legitimate need for such information and to whom the organization has authorized disclosure. Board and staff members shall use confidential information solely for the purpose of performing services as a trustee or employee for Northside. This policy is not intended to prevent disclosure where it is required by law.

Board and staff members must exercise good judgment and care at all times to avoid unauthorized or improper disclosure of confidential information. Conversations in public places, such as dining facilities, elevators, or hallways, should be limited to matters that are not of a sensitive or confidential nature. In addition, board and staff members should be sensitive to the risks of inadvertent disclosure and should refrain from leaving confidential information on desks or otherwise in plain view. They should also refrain from using such things as speaker phones to discuss confidential information if the conversations could be heard by unauthorized persons.

At the end of a trustee's term in office or upon the termination of an employee's employment, he or she shall return all documents, papers, or other material, regardless of medium, that may contain confidential information.

and preferences, if known or reasonably assessed, should guide clinical decisions.

The problem with this standard is that, more times than not, we do not have such conversations; therefore, surrogates and providers often cannot say they know with reasonable certainty what a particular patient wants. It is critically important for the board to ensure that health care providers are skilled at having these conversations—because it is impossible to document discussions that have never taken place. However, when it comes to having conversations with patients or their surrogates about the impending death of a patient, the first problem is getting those interactions to happen at all. But they must: a typical oncologist has to deliver news of terminal illness an average of thirty-five times a month.

Yet some physicians and nurses believe they must go to heroic extremes to avoid death. Add to that a litigious society that seeks to assign blame for all unhappy events, and one has the recipe for the kind of death, and its aftermath, experienced by Susan, Edith, and their father (see chapter 3). Surely, we can do better than that. The ethics of Hippocratic medicine stress that physicians should not continue to treat aggressively when the disease has "overmastered" the patient. If a moral consensus has been reached by the treating team (perhaps not to start dialysis, not to reinsert the feeding tube, or only to provide comfort measures), the possibility of legal action should not make the risk managers or attorneys put pressure on the team to provide what they consider to be ethically inappropriate or ineffective care. Efforts to bring the patient or patient's surrogate fully into the decision-making process will occur in facilities where the board members and administrators create an ethical climate conducive to such emotionally taxing discussions.

Medical Mistakes

End-of-life care is not the only dramatic situation in which the ethical climate of a hospital can make a difference in a clinician's behavior. The whole arena of medical mistakes, highlighted by the Institute of Medicine's (IOM's) comprehensive report *To Err Is Human,* is another.[1] Medical mistakes and how they are addressed once they occur determine how a hospital nourishes or deadens its internal processes for making ethical decisions. Although boards delegate quality-of-care review and improvement to the medical and supporting hospital staff, the board remains fully responsible for the oversight of those activities. Yet this process varies depending on the way in which the medical staff and the hospital staff view their respective roles in evaluating and improving the quality and safety of care.

After presenting the following case, we'll look at the broad issue of medical mistakes and the power invested in the health care hierarchy.

Case 4-3. An Early Vacation

A patient was operated on for an aneurysm. At the end of the procedure, there appeared to be unexplained, continued blood loss. The surgeon's assistant finished closing the wound, and the surgeon left the operating room and then left town for the weekend. The patient was taken to the ICU and was found to have profound hypotension (low blood pressure). The patient went into cardiac arrest and died. Subsequently, it was determined that he died because he lost blood from the aneurysm repair. The medical staff evaluated the surgeon, but during the evaluation the surgeon moved to another city to begin a new practice. The medical staff evaluation determined that the surgeon made a poor judgment in the case but did not recommend a report to the board of medical examiners nor a report to the board of trustees. A letter to the surgeon simply stated that the case had been reviewed.

Questions for discussion:

1. What are the ethical issues at stake with this situation? How should they be weighed?
2. What should the board of trustees do?
3. Did the medical staff members fulfill their obligation regarding peer review and quality of care?
4. What guidelines or policies should the board set to deal with such situations in the future?

Although the reader may be thinking that this kind of mistake must be very rare, nothing could be further from the truth. According to the IOM report, published in 2000, preventable adverse events—an injury resulting from medical management—are alarmingly high. The IOM report estimates that preventable adverse events may result in as many as 98,000 deaths annually. This statistic makes medical error a leading cause of death in the United States, exceeding deaths caused by motor vehicle accidents and breast cancer.

In case 4-3, a constellation of problems resulted in the error. But this case highlights an especially important problem that the medical community needs to address openly and explicitly: the medical power hierarchy.

Medicine has long been a vertically controlled domain. Many nurses remember when they had to stand in the presence of a physician and were simply expected to carry out physician orders without question. Today, such subservience would be considered both unprofessional and insulting. But the inclination to be deferential to the physician on all matters related to the care of patients continues. There is a psychological need on the part of patients to believe that their physicians are all knowing and good, caring people.

Without questioning the belief that clinicians are good and caring people, both the medical profession and the public need to change their frame of reference. Medicine is as much an art as it is a science. We believe that clinicians and the public need to openly and explicitly acknowledge, and adjust to, the complexity and general uncertainty that is the art of practicing medicine. The singular relationship of physician and patient has been transformed into team medicine, teams on which there is often cultural and social diversity. And if this shift is to work well, a process that builds team consensus must replace the old top-down methods of decision making. Only through the formal actions of board members and administrative leaders can such a major change occur.

In the surgery case cited above, there are issues involving the actions of the surgeon and the assistant, the concerns of the operating room staff members, and the relationship between the medical staff and the board. On the surface, it appears that the medical staff members may not have fulfilled their obligation regarding quality of care (that is, the peer review process). The board delegates its obligation for quality of care to those groups that have sufficient knowledge and experience to assess and monitor quality of care. One of those groups is the medical staff. The board relies heavily on the medical staff to perform this function, and the board must develop a relationship that allows it to know that the medical staff performs this function well. In the example above, the board may wonder whether the medical staff members have been performing their duties as well as they should. Again, how should the board approach this issue? What are the ethical issues involved?

Fair Financial Practices

Another example of an issue that has the potential for strengthening or weakening trust in the facility and its mission is related to the reuse of clinical equipment. Case 4-4 illustrates this issue.

Case 4-4. Reusing "Single Use Only" Equipment

Dr. Jones from the cardiac catheterization laboratory calls the director of your hospital's ethics committee about an equipment issue. The concerns are about pricing and information disclosure to patients. In the cath lab, the practice of reusing a special part of the cardiac catheterization equipment is longstanding. That is, a particular piece of the heart catheter, on which the manufacturer has stamped "Single Use Only," is not being thrown away after its use in a patient. It is sterilized and reused.

Dr. Jones wonders if other "Single Use Only" items are being reused in other departments in your hospital. This may be a nationwide practice. In addition, the way the "Single Use Only" items are prepared for reuse varies. Some items are sterilized and prepared for reuse in-house. Others go to companies that specialize in medical refurbishing. These companies reprocess and repackage the sterilized items before they are returned essentially new, or so these companies contend.

Although concerned about the safety questions raised by this practice in the cath lab, Dr. Jones is not raising the issue on that basis. The practice is longstanding, and there is no evidence of safety problems. Rather, the issue has come up in the context of fraud and compliance. Patients are being charged the price for new devices, whether or not the item is reused.

Questions for discussion:

1. Is this unfair pricing?
2. What are the ethical issues at stake in this matter?
3. What, if anything, should patients and physicians be told about reuse?
4. Should the price charged to the insurer be different depending on whether the patient received a new or reused device?
5. Should the board address these questions and formulate a policy on reuse? What would be important components of such a policy?

Reuse of clinical equipment is a widespread practice about which the public usually knows nothing. It is also an issue that produces a visceral reaction such as, "They want to put something in me that's been in someone else?" Therefore, how the hospital establishes policies and procedures related to the reuse of medical instruments ought to be handled in such a way that, if scrutinized by others, it will appear thoughtful and fair. This is a perfect issue for the board's involvement in ethics.

A Matter of Justice, Not Just Compliance

Amid heightened concerns about fraud and abuse audits, cardiac catheterization departments have become aware of the potential for charges of improper billing related to reprocessed instruments. Often patients are charged the new-instrument price whether the instrument has been reprocessed or not. But this is not only a compliance concern. The following questions of justice arise:

- Is there fairness and equity in patient costs?
- Do some patients receive preferential treatment because their physician knows to ask for an unused device?

- What information should be disclosed to patients about the differences between new and reprocessed instruments?

These are important questions of clinical and organizational ethics. There are valid reasons to use reprocessed equipment in the cath lab. And it is not clear whether there are any increased safety problems with these reprocessed instruments. But even if there are no serious safety and operational issues involved in reusing an instrument stamped "Single Use Only" by the manufacturer, there are other facets of reprocessing to consider. For example, there are no FDA criteria differentiating what must be stamped "Single Use Only" and what need not carry such a stamp. It is clearly to the manufacturer's financial advantage to have hospitals buy new equipment for each patient and each procedure. The board's involvement in this issue will help define the answers to important questions, such as the following:

- Which specific items should be marked "Single Use Only"?
- Are in-house sterilization procedures sufficient?
- Is outsourcing deemed acceptable?
- What information should be shared with patients?
- How should the hospital bill patients, insurance companies, and government payers?

Helping Patients with Their Bill

A policy that calls for patients to be responsible for their own bill is reasonable. How the policy is carried out, however, may be quite unreasonable. Policies often state that the patient is responsible for the costs of care; once the hospital has provided the patient with a bill, from the hospital's perspective that should be that. However, it is critically important that institutional policies be written with sufficient elasticity to accommodate the untidiness of the world outside the hospital walls. Billing is a perfect example of hospital operations that should be efficiently organized. But efficiency is not synonymous with effectiveness. In fact, the most effective systems may be those that build sufficient flexibility into efficient operations so that the variability of the real world can be addressed smoothly.

Let's consider how a hospital might organize its billing policies and procedures to meet its goals of getting paid fully and promptly without frustrating its patients or its own billing clerks. Although a policy might say that "patients are responsible for their bills," an additional piece could add: "When our patients are covered by third-party insurers (including public funding), we will assist them in obtaining payment for covered services." This might, at first, look like a big task for the hospital. But if it appears overwhelming to a hospital, think what it is like for patients, some perhaps still quite ill, to work through the morass of paper and regulations related to insurance coverage.

There are numerous creative ways for a hospital to provide assistance. At the first sign of difficulty, the hospital could provide the patient with the name and telephone number of the insurance company or government customer-service department. The hospital could go even further by calling the insurer and assisting to clarify the problem. It is in the hospital's self-interest to help payments get processed. If problems persist, the hospital can have a volunteer help the patient get the payment processed. Procedural flexibility would allow direct billing after two failed attempts. Optimally, the hospital's department heads would discuss billing and collection problems at their meetings. A summary could then be sent to the board on a regular basis.

In any organization, quality depends on employees' taking responsibility for solving problems. It becomes the board's role to ensure that rules and policies are constructive, not barriers to sound practice. When rules and policies support high-quality operations, staff members feel empowered to move toward more excellent performance.

Integrity and Organizational Character

Is there such a thing as organizational character? Organizational behaviorists have explored the impact of internal operating cultures on employee performance. How does the culture of a system define its character? The federal government and state governments devote less effort to documenting excellence in practice than in trying to ferret out fraud and abuse. Such audits call the organization's character into question. "Character is all we have," asserted a hospital president in the Southeast. Allegations of fraud and waste must be taken seriously, but the standards against which the government conducts reviews are no clearer than the statutory language, regulations, and court cases needed to interpret them. Thus, honest errors occur that should never be called "fraud." Hospitals need policies to show how internal operations are always subject to continuous review and improvement.

Boards must ensure that needed internal controls are in place before external reviews begin. Like the proverbial barn door, it is too late to institute controls when the green visors arrive! These problems arise in part because even the fiscal intermediaries will not give answers to billing questions; they accept legal advice not to render an opinion in order to cover their legal liabilities. This compels the hospital to make the best guesses possible. The problem is that the decision makers often are well-trained billing clerks who must interpret hundreds of pages of laws, thousands of pages of regulations, and decisions on a specific topic. Well-meaning staff members sometimes reach different conclusions than auditors do months and years later. Once institutional integrity has been questioned, it is hard to earn it back, even if the audit is clean. Honest mistakes are not "fraud and abuse."

As an example, Medicare may pay $25 for a physician visit, whereas a patient's private insurance will cover up to $100 for the same visit. Even the barber who rents space in the hospital is paid more than this and does not have the same level of regulation, paperwork, and accreditation to worry about! Is it any wonder some providers opt to refer rather than accept Medicare patients? Yet hospitals do not have that choice. As the disparity between cost of providing services and reimbursement grows, the conflict between physicians and hospitals also grows. When the cost for chemotherapy drugs exceeds the reimbursement from Medicare or other sources of payment (including the patient), the hospital is generally looked to as the provider. As in an earlier example, this may create a constant drain on the resources of the hospital, which may threaten the hospital's ability to provide care to the community. Discussions about this conflict must occur before a crisis develops.

Board members should be briefed on the annual audit, including the management letter that usually accompanies the financial statement. Management letters inform the organizational leaders of possible problems in their internal procedures, control, security, and documentation, assist compliance with government and professional standards, and prevent problems in the future.

Managing system finances and accountability is one way to maintain integrity and character. Another is to prevent conflicts of interest. In some ways, the appearance of a conflict can undermine public trust and erode an institution's culture as much as the actual conflict. Chapter 5 focuses on how boards can respond to both real and apparent conflicts of interest.

Reference

1. Institute of Medicine, Committee on Quality of Health Care in America (L. T. Kohn, J. M. Corrigan, and M. S. Donaldson, eds.), *To Err Is Human: Building a Safer Health System* (Washington, D.C.: National Academy Press, 2000).

5

Exercising Ethical Leadership

W HAT DOES the successful organizational ethical program and culture look like? If board members can understand what the ideal is, it becomes easier for them to work toward that aspiration. A good ethical culture, however, is not a utopia. The differences between the two become apparent in the types of cases that have worked their way to the board and the ethics committees. These cases often focused on which patients were given access, or denied access, to limited resources (such as a dialysis machine). Such heart-wrenching choices required a new model of decision making, and as a result of court cases and decisions on accreditation, the health care field saw the emergence of ethics committees.

Their arrival heralded a new era of institutional ethics, although at the time people probably did not realize it. The paternalism of the providers' recommendations yielded to a committee's review and recommendations. These task groups were composed of people who had otherwise been excluded from the decision-making process. Thus the people within the committee structure had become part of the solution.

This chapter explores a variety of situations that define ethical culture and processes. The major emphasis here is on the broad issues raised by conflicts of interest—those that actually occur and those that have the appearance of conflicting interests. Beyond these issues are the ethical concerns raised by managed care, the relationship between an institution's staff and the drug companies, and the rise of commercialism through advertising. Case examples illustrate the complexity of the issues. Given the variety of services, programs, and professional and business connections in contemporary health systems, each board will reach its own conclusions. The actual decisions are important; having the foundations to reach those decisions is critical.

Sometimes the ethical issues come to the fore in the emergency room. How do staff members deal with the disruptive patient? For the institution, the central question: Do the concepts of respect for individual rights and treating all patients with respect remain in the minds of the staff members when that patient is experiencing pain and lashing out at anyone who will listen? Aristotle notes that we become what we repeatedly do. Alternatively, we repeatedly do what is consistent with who we are and with our values and beliefs.

Board members bring many different skills and areas of expertise with them. These skills and knowledge are often extremely helpful to the board (physicians may provide insight into complex clinical issues; corporate leaders may provide insight into business planning), but those same qualities may place the individual trustee in a position of possible conflict of interest. Let's test these ideas with the following case.

Case 5-1. Upgrading the Computers

Jack is a trustee and, as the CEO of a local high-tech firm, is knowledgeable about computers. It is time to have a major overhaul of the computer equipment in the surgery, trauma, and burn units. Jack offers to talk with the medical chiefs and nursing supervisors in those departments to lend his expertise; he also visits departments of hospitals around the state that have recently upgraded their systems. Having identified four companies that appear to meet the hospital's needs, Jack has offered suggestions about the best suppliers.

One of the vendors calls him and asks to come over to discuss the needs of the hospital in greater detail in preparation for the proposal. The vendor tells Jack of a meeting the vendor is having for its other hospital users and invites Jack to attend. The vendor suggests that this would be a good way for Jack to talk with other hospital representatives who use the vendor's computers for the same purposes; he also mentions that the meeting is being held at a resort where Jack can get in a little golf. What does Jack do?

Questions for discussion:

1. What should Jack do? Why?
2. Which of the basic principles does this case raise?
3. In what ways might some or all of these principles conflict?
4. What policies should the board put in place to guide responses to such situations?

Previously in this book, three traditional theories of ethical analysis were introduced; one of these was duty-based ethical theory. The central tenet of duty-based ethics is that the way to determine whether an action is right or good is by determining whether the people performing that action have met their duties and obligations. Yet it is often difficult to sort through and separate out one's duties and obligations. Failing to clarify, separate, or appropriately manage these duties and obligations causes potential conflicts of interest.

Conflicts of Interest

To ensure the institution as a whole, and the board in particular, appreciate the need to ferret out and create mechanisms to manage conflicts of interest, it is necessary that we develop useful definitions of conflicts of interest. See figure 5-1 for an example of such policy. This policy declares that the core ethical duty of a hospital is to put the care of its patients first, with no conflicts of interest.

Board members have a legal duty of loyalty to the organization, which is putting the interests of the organization above their personal interests. They demonstrate this by avoiding conflicts of interest and disclosing any potential conflicts of interest that might exist.

Board members and employees must abide by conflict-of-interest policies. These policies should make clear what the term *conflict of interest* means, what individuals must do to disclose possible conflicts of interest, and what they should do to avoid acting inappropriately in a conflict-of-interest situation. Recent regulations of the Internal Revenue Service provide ways to punish those who violate standards of conduct. For example, sanctions apply to

Figure 5-1.   Conflict-of-Interest Policy of Northside Health Care Network

Board members and staff members have obligations to conduct business within guidelines that prohibit actual or potential conflicts of interest. This policy establishes only the framework within which Northside Health Care Network intends to carry out its work. The purpose of these guidelines is to provide general direction so that trustees and staff members can seek further clarification of issues related to the subject of acceptable standards of operation.

An actual or potential conflict of interest occurs when anyone is in a position to influence a decision that may result in a personal gain for that person, or for any relative or business associate of that person, as a result of Northside's business dealings. For the purpose of this policy, a relative is any person who is related by blood or marriage to a Northside trustee or staff member, and a business associate is any person who has any business relationship through outside organizations that have or may have contractual links with Northside.

No presumption of guilt is created by the mere existence of a relationship with outside firms. However, if any Northside trustee or staff member has any influence on transactions involving purchases, contracts, or leases, it is imperative that she or he disclose to an officer of the organization as soon as possible the existence of any actual or potential conflict of interest so that safeguards can be established to protect all parties.

Personal gain may result not only in situations where a trustee or employee or relative or associate has a significant ownership in a firm with which Northside does business but also when any person receives any kickback, substantial gift, or special consideration as a result of any transaction of business dealings involving Northside.

The material, products, designs, plans, ideas, and data of Northside are the sole property of this organization and should never be given to any outside firm or individual except through normal channels and with appropriate authorization. Any improper transfer of material or disclosure of information, even though it is not apparent that the trustee or employee has personally gained by such action, constitutes unacceptable conduct. Anyone who participates in such a practice shall be subject to disciplinary action up to and including discharge.

The ethics committee of the board oversees this policy and ensures compliance with it and all matters related to ethical behavior.

"excess benefit transactions" and impose stiff penalties on board and senior staff leaders who are in positions to influence financial decisions.

A policy on conflict of interest provides guidance in any circumstance in which the organization is considering entering into a transaction or arrangement that might benefit the private interests (especially financial) of a trustee or any relative, business associate, or corporation linked to the trustee. A financial interest is not necessarily a conflict of interest, but it may be. Voting on one's own compensation would be as much a conflict of interest as owning shares in a company bidding for a contract with the organization.

Full disclosure of all material facts is essential before the board considers any proposed transaction or arrangement. That person should then be excused from discussions determining whether a conflict is present and how to deal with it. The board may appoint a disinterested person or group to investigate alternatives to the proposed transaction to see if a more advantageous arrangement for the organization may be available elsewhere. Decisions must promote the organization's best interests and benefits and be fair and reasonable on its behalf.

If a board has cause to believe that a member has failed to disclose actual or possible conflicts of interest, it should inform that person of the basis for that belief and provide an opportunity to explain the situation. If the explanation is not satisfactory, the board should take appropriate disciplinary and corrective action.

The board should also record in its minutes the names of the person(s) who disclosed or were otherwise found to have a financial interest in connection with a possible or actual conflict, the nature of that interest, any action taken to determine if an actual conflict was present, and the board's decision regarding whether a conflict of interest existed. The record should include the names of trustees participating in these discussions and votes, the content of the discussions, the alternatives considered to the proposed transaction, and the vote(s) taken.

Each board member should annually sign statements that he or she has received and read a copy of the board's conflict-of-interest policy, agreed to comply with it fully, and recorded any potential conflicts in advance. A board committee on ethics could oversee this process.

Conflicts of Commitment

It is virtually impossible to live an active and full life experience without making difficult choices. When you are a trustee, board activities may interfere with your other obligations, such as your job or spending time with your family. How you parse out the conflicts among these interests takes a measure of courage. It is difficult to tell your boss that you cannot stay late for a meeting because you promised to have dinner with your spouse, and it would not be fair to break that obligation a third time for work. It may be even harder to tell your five-year-old child that you will not make a birthday party because you have to give a work-related presentation out of town.

These examples are conflicts of commitment, a set of conditions in which primary interests are in tension. For example, hospital physicians have commitments to serve on committees needed to run the hospital properly. Although the roles of clinician, teacher, and participant in organizational activities may collide, physicians can be expected to prioritize their time to give all three the needed attention. However the balance is struck, the primacy of care of the patient is rarely, if ever, threatened. When money is added into the mix, however, conflicts often arise.

When conflicting interests become conflicts of interests, they require board consideration and review. Whether a hospital has for-profit or nonprofit tax status, both need money to operate. An institution simply cannot function for long without generating income. But how that money is generated should always be of interest and concern to the board. In reviewing various income streams, the board must be alert to possible conflicts of interest. One example is the way large sums of money are generated by hospitals and medical centers through sponsored research. This brings us to the Gelsinger case.

Case 5-2. Jesse Gelsinger Is Dead

"In the case of:

John Gelsinger as Administrator and Personal Representative of the Estate of Jesse Gelsinger and Paul Gelsinger, in his own right: Plaintiffs

"The Trustees of the University of Pennsylvania, James Wilson, M.D., Genovo, Inc., Steven Raper, M.D., Mark Batshaw, M.D., William Kelley, M.D., Children's Hospital of Philadelphia, Children's National Medical Center, and Arthur Caplan, Ph.D.: Defendants

"This is not an arbitration matter; assessment of damages hearing is required. Jury trial of twelve (12) persons is hereby demanded."[1]

Jesse Gelsinger was an eighteen-year-old man with the rare genetic metabolic disorder, ornithine transcarbamylase deficiency (OTC). He is said to have had a mild form of the disorder, which was controlled by a low-protein diet and drugs, and he led a reasonably normal life. Jesse became a research volunteer in a study conducted at the University of Pennsylvania's (UPENN's) Institute for Human Gene Therapy (IHGT), investigating OTC gene transfer. Jesse died while in the research study. There has been no disagreement that Jesse died as a result of the administration of the experimental drug.

In the court papers it has been claimed that:

1. Dr. Wilson, the principal investigator of the study in which Jesse died, was the founder of Genovo, the company developing the experimental agent that was injected into Jesse and that caused Jesse's death.

2. Dr. Wilson controlled up to 30 percent of the Genovo stock during the relevant time period.

3. Genovo had agreed to provide the IHGT more than $4 million per year for five years to conduct genetic research and experimentation prior to the study's being initiated.

4. In return for Genovo's support of genetic research, UPENN agreed to give Genovo licenses for lung and liver applications for existing technologies developed by Dr. Wilson and the ability to negotiate for other possible licenses for applications developed by Dr. Wilson in the future.

5. Genovo shareholders included numerous past and present UPENN and/or IHGT employees, including Dr. Steven Raper, Mark Batshaw, and Dr. William Kelley.

6. Dr. Arthur Caplan, director of the bioethics department, trustee professor of bioethics in the department of molecular and cellular engineering, UPENN, was consulted about the design and ethical complexities posed by the study in which Jesse died.

7. The IHGT agreed to give approximately $25,000 in support of a bioethics faculty position.

After the settlement was reached, it turned out that the principal investigator, Dr. Wilson, and at least several of his colleagues had serious conflicts of interest.

Questions for discussion:

1. What ethical issues are present in this situation?
2. In what ways are conflicts of interest affecting the participants?
3. What should the board of UPENN have done?
4. What policies would you suggest to that board so it avoids such situations in the future?

Conflict of interest may be in the eye of the beholder. When attempting to identify a conflict of interest, one is reminded of the words of U.S. Supreme Court Justice Potter Stewart: "I might not be able to define pornography, but I know it when I see it."

Attempts to clarify just what constitutes a conflict of interest in human subject research have been made for many years. Some draw their definitions from biblical sources: "No one can serve two masters, for either he will hate the one and love the other, or he will be devoted to one and despise the other" (Matthew 6:24). Other definitions include the following from a book on biomedical research:

A person with a conflict of interest has two masters to serve, and these two masters do not always have coincident needs. Scientific motivations are not always in conflict when two masters are

served. When the two masters appear to have coincident interests, then the conflict may best be described as a potential conflict of interest. Theoretically, at least, the two masters must have
divergent interests in the same endeavor for conflict to be present. Investigators who wish to downplay a conflict of interest in
their research often refer to the serving of two masters as a
"potential" problem; others may simply call it a "conflict of
interest."[2]

If one is generous, rather than calling the conflicting interests of
pursuing scientific ends and protecting individual subjects as a bona
fide conflict of interest, one might think of these as conflicts of commitment like the conflicts presented by balancing family, work, and
civic obligations. At the very least, the potential for conflicts of commitment may pressure patients to become research subjects. The
responsibility of the hospital's governing body is to protect patient
welfare by stating that patient care requirements outweigh research
protocols.

One clear conflict is between meeting the goals of science to create new knowledge and protecting the rights and welfare of subjects.[3] Because the amount of money flowing to academic and
community hospitals for sponsored research has increased markedly
over the last several decades, public scrutiny of this conflict has
intensified.[4] Tragedies like the death of Jesse Gelsinger raise concerns about the coercive effects of money on institutional integrity.[5]
Such conflicts can no longer be hidden under the rubric of *potential*
problems. The financial interest requires that the accurate term is
now, quite definitely, *conflict of interest* and that this conflict of
interest be squarely addressed.[6] In fact, financial conflicts have
become so stark that Donna Shalala, Ph.D., as secretary of the U.S.
Department of Health and Human Services, proposed federal legis-
lation to levy penalties of up to $250,000 per clinical investigator
and up to $1 million per institution for violations of ethical human
subjects research practices.[7]

A succinct and explicit definition by D. F. Thompson in the *New
England Journal of Medicine* may be the most explanatory: "A conflict of interest is a set of conditions in which professional judgment

concerning a primary interest (such as a patient's welfare or the validity of research) tends to be unduly influenced by a secondary interest (such as financial gain)."[8]

This definition is particularly appealing, as the term *unduly influenced* is linguistically and conceptually close to the regulatory language of undue influence. Institutional review boards (IRBs) are required by law to protect research subjects against such influences. But doing so takes courage, especially when it means possibly reducing the institution's potential income. This becomes obvious in the following case.

Case 5-3. Century's Connections

Century Health Care System's active research program includes one of the most prestigious cardiac surgery programs in its region. This program serves the hospital system in many ways. Because of its reputation for excellence, it regularly attracts top new cardiac surgeons from across the country. Patients fly in from all corners of the globe to have surgery performed by the cardiac surgery group, which conducts its own single-site trials and participates in many multicenter trials. These trials attract large sums of sponsored research grants. A cardiac stent protocol has come to the hospital. It is the fourth such protocol the IRB has reviewed this year. Inclusion and exclusion criteria for all these protocols are relatively similar, as are the experimental aspects of the protocols. Minor differences in stint placement and materials are being examined.

Questions for discussion:

1. What are the ethical issues at stake in this situation?
2. How should the board of this organization deal with it?
3. How well is your own organization prepared to deal with such situations?

The IRB members should ask how potential subjects are being directed to one protocol or another. They need to know the research budget and whether any money is going directly to the investigators.

The IRB wants to know how much money the institution is receiving for each of the existing protocols and for the newest one that is being reviewed by the IRB. And the IRB wants to know if any of the investigators or other employees have any equity, consulting, or other potential financial interest in any of the sponsoring companies.

This situation highlights the need for IRBs and the governing board to become increasingly vigilant about sources of conflicts of interest. IRBs are not used to asking questions about financial conflicts of interest of investigators and are even less accustomed to asking about institutional conflicts of interest. But ask they must! And the institutions must have policies in place to respond to the IRB and anyone else who has a legitimate right to learn about an institution's and an investigator's financial ties to research money. Otherwise, their ability to ensure the highest-quality patient care is compromised.

Conflict-of-interest issues are frequently cited in situations in which those conflicts may be more apparent than real. The following case study raises several issues for the board, one of which is a perception of possible conflicts of interest.

Case 5-4. Real Estate

In 1999 your hospital determined, through a process of strategic planning, that an off-site clinic near the area of growth of your city would be helpful in serving the community. As a result, your hospital purchased real estate for the new clinic. In 2000, again through an extensive strategic-planning process, your organization determined that an off-site clinic was not needed (a group of physicians had developed a clinic near the area you had thought needed medical services) and therefore the real estate was no longer needed. You listed the real estate with an agent who promised to sell the property promptly. Several years have passed and there have been no viable offers for the property. Your hospital needs cash to purchase new equipment. One of your board members is the best commercial real estate broker in the area, and she offers to sell the property.

Questions for discussion:

1. What, if any, are the issues involved in accepting her offer?
2. What ethical principles are at stake in this situation, and what should such policies include?
3. How should the board frame policies about decisions in such situations to avoid conflicts of interest and maintain public trust and accountability?

Even when there is no true conflict of interest, the situation may appear to those outside the boardroom to be one in which there is a conflict, with possible personal gain. In these situations, the board must either err on the side of avoiding such apparent conflicts or be extremely proactive in its public explanation of the value to the organization of the particular action. Without this public disclosure and discussion, the public may well decide that the organization is not acting in the best interest of its patients and stakeholders.

Managed Care

The ethical complexities of human subject research and the opportunities research presents for serious conflicts of interest are not the only source of such conflicts. As Thompson's definition suggests, conflicts of interest can surface within strictly clinical situations as well. It was predicted several years ago that "conflicts of interest will become central to the day-to-day business of the ethics consultant and ethics committee."[9] This prediction is coming true. Sometimes the managed care approach seems to conflict with patient care, as illustrated in case 5-5.

Case 5-5. Family or Financial Gain

You are the chief medical officer and have just met with one of the new physicians in your HMO. Dr. Janet Smith recently completed her residency program and settled into a new home with her new husband and young baby. She would like to practice her medical specialty, which is internal medicine, within a reasonably normal work schedule so she can see her young daughter grow up and have time to spend with her husband. She agreed to join your HMO as a staff physician. Although she is paid less than her colleagues who join private practice groups, she feels it is a reasonable trade-off, given her ability to maintain a five-day-a-week, nine-to-five schedule, with few weekend or evening calls. What troubles her, however, is that the contract she has signed restricts her ability to make patient referrals to other specialists or hospitals. Most troubling is that she will receive raises and bonuses based on the efficiency with which she can provide patient care.

Questions for discussion:

1. What ethical issues are at stake in this situation?
2. What do you recommend the doctor do?
3. To whom can she raise these issues?
4. Is this an issue you should bring to the board's attention?
5. What policies should the board formulate to guide responses to such situations?

A basic tenet of managed care is to minimize the amount of unnecessary or unwarranted testing and treatment while maximizing the effectiveness of the care delivered. An apparent conflict of interest may arise when a physician does not order tests or medications that the patient feels are indicated (and the patient may feel they are not ordered because of economic pressures). An argument can be made that the patients knew the managed care plan they selected was based on these tenets and that they gave their consent to that limitation; but it is unlikely that they were informed of the fact that their physicians directly benefited from limiting service.

These are examples of ethical tensions and conflicts of interest that the managed care system poses for physicians. Practicing as a physician and maintaining a family life means balancing conflicts of commitment. Therefore, the corporate world of the HMO is a reasonable solution. But corporate medicine carries with it the inherent tension of serving two masters. As a physician, one has the fiduciary responsibility to the patient. As a staff member of an HMO, one has obligations to protect its financial ability to provide appropriate care to its member patients. As if this tension were not hard enough to manage, financial incentives and rewards to provide highly efficient (some would say too efficient) care add a bona fide conflict of interest. To address such conflicts takes courage on the part of both physician staff and corporate boards. Hospitals and HMOs should develop policies to protect patients from the problems posed by such conflicts.

Drug Incentives

Another potential conflict in today's health care system lies in the relationship between physicians and the pharmaceutical industry. ABC News estimated in 1999 that the drug companies were spending an average of $3,000 per physician to market their products. The financial stakes are enormous. Should a hospital or university medical center allow a doctor to accept free trips to resorts to hear the latest results of unpublished research paid for by that manufacturer? Should the physician inform a patient of this connection when prescribing that firm's product? Does the institution absolve itself of any conflict by accepting "free" samples of that firm's drugs for distribution to its indigent patients? Does the public believe the hospital is not compromising one insured patient's care so it can help hundreds of others who lack insurance? Because such issues arise with increasing frequency, the organization needs a mechanism to resolve the inevitable debates.

We believe the traditional ethics committee is not the appropriate locus for such debates. The patient ethics committee is mandated to look at individual doctor-patient relationships. Rather, as this book demonstrates, the board needs to work in concert with the CEO to develop a separate organizational ethics structure, process, and conversation. As we have explored in this chapter, silence will not resolve conflicts of interest or the appearance of such conflicts.

Advertising

Advertising may create conflicts of interest as it becomes more common in the health care industry. Although it has important ethical implications, advertising is not a patient care issue that is easily addressed within the traditional ethics committee. Although there are guidelines available, most advertisements try to be "informative" or "educational." Rarely do ads cast negative messages about competitors, although it does occasionally happen. The board should actively ensure that programs and services used in an advertising campaign can indeed be delivered. There is no room for bait-and-switch tactics in medicine. This obligation extends to employees for their own protection as well as for that of the community.

Connected to this issue are the myriad services and programs that the institution chooses *not* to advertise. Many hospitals downplay the amount of indigent (and therefore unreimbursed) care they give. If it's simply because they don't want to brag, then it is an appropriate tactic and strategy. If, on the other hand, the administration fears a wave of poor clients using their clinics or emergency room services, then the board should actively enter the discussion. Is the failure to educate the public in this instance a subtle form of rationing by withholding information?

Implications for the Board

Disclosing conflicts of interest is a moral and public relations necessity. Yet it is not clear what must be disclosed and through what means. Therefore, boards need to develop policies addressing disclosure of conflicts of interest. In so doing, the board needs to determine just what it thinks about clarifying, separating, and disclosing conflicts of interest.

There are varying notions about just how far one must go to avoid conflicts of interest. Some believe that all such conflicts should be eradicated. For example, if a physician-investigator owns stock in a company that produces a drug or device that person is researching, then the physician-investigator must sell that equity interest. Furthermore, such a physician-investigator cannot be a consultant to, or be an officer of, such a corporation.

The problem with going to this length to limit conflicts of interest is that there are many health-related products and services being developed by companies set up by the only persons who are professionally capable of producing and researching those drugs or devices. This situation arises because many promising researchers simply cannot obtain sufficient nonprofit research funding and must seek venture capital to advance the research. Once such companies are set up, it is almost impossible to separate science from corporate relationships.

Disclosure of such entangled and financial incentives may not be enough to protect the public from the combined press of the scientific imperative and the patients' need for improved treatments. Thus, mechanisms for establishing firewalls, on top of explicit and frank disclosure, are being discussed. For example, one measure that can easily be taken is to have someone other than a researcher or provider with a financial interest at stake implement the formal informed-consent procedures. Furthermore, nonaffiliated physicians can be employed to monitor patient safety and welfare.

In the strictly clinical arena, especially in the managed care environment, trustees must take seriously the institution's responsibility to place patient care first. This responsibility requires critical examination of all contracts with clinicians and vendors to ensure that revenue and income projections do not place patients at risk.

The Nominating Committee

Each board committee must have a clear mandate and agreed-upon annual tasks. Often the committee's work in one year repeats what it did the year before without connecting it to the overall needs of the board or institution. Let's examine the nominating committee to see how these changes might occur.

For years, hospital boards of trustees had ethical postures that developed from neglect, passivity, and silence. Seats on the board were often a tangible reward for continuing philanthropy. The argument was simple and straightforward: the individuals who donated the money had an interest in the institution and its progress. This model has been prevalent in orchestras, museums, United Way agencies, and religious organizations. It is a visible and overt way of supporting the hospital. It can be seen as an outgrowth of the competitive marketplace for nonprofit giving.

At its core, trusteeship for donations hopes to gain caring, responsible, trustworthy, and wise donors. That system worked fairly well for most of the twentieth century. Many health care organizations would not have been able to achieve their community prominence without such charitable giving. Our tax laws encouraged it, hospitals needed it, individuals benefited from it, and the community had a needed resource. It was a symbiotic relationship.

But times have changed. The growth of public programs, especially Medicare and Medicaid, and the expansion of private health insurance have reduced the relative impact of philanthropy as part of the hospital's revenue.

The board's nominating committee often ends its work when nominees are approved for membership on the board. But what would happen if the committee's charge were expanded to include activities through the new trustees' first year of service? The nominating committee could be responsible for ensuring the new trustee receives and understands all policies, has a sense of the organization's physical structure, and has a liaison or mentor to call for further information, advice, and education.

Let's dream a bit. What if the nominating committee were reconceptualized as the trustee development committee, charged with ongoing board education, trustee needs assessment, and planning sessions to develop the board and its effectiveness. These are active roles far beyond filling empty seats at the board conference table.

Ethics Committees and Institutional Review Boards

What if some board members also serve on the hospital ethics committee? Why couldn't trustees sit on the IRB in academic medical centers, which seek to combine care and research as central elements of their mission? What prevents ethics committee chairs from making reports and leading board seminars on the major issues they confront during the year?

The facility needs to assure the board that someone has clear responsibility for the operation of the IRB as well as for the institutional animal use and care committee. Members of the legal staff often make similar presentations on liability issues. Some critics might view this model of trustee involvement in the major decisions as an intrusion or as micromanagement. Indeed, it could become that. But the trade-off is an informed, active board rather than a rubber stamp. Boards often affirm institutional decisions by default because they endorsed the process. But the content of the decisions and actions must also be in alignment with the organization's policies, strategy, and values. Case 5-6 illustrates that alignment (or possible lack of it).

Case 5-6. CEO Evaluation

It is the expressed policy of the board to evaluate the CEO's performance annually. For some reason this requirement has not been fulfilled for the past two years. The hospital is running smoothly and operating in the black. Patient satisfaction surveys have been consistently positive, and the hospital continues to receive good local media attention.

Questions for discussion:

1. Does it really matter that board policy requires annual CEO evaluations?
2. What risks are there for inaction?
3. What would you say if this issue occurred at your next board meeting?

As Pamela Hemann wrote in *Board Member:* "There are two key responsibilities of the board chair. First, the chair must work with the chief executive to keep the board focused on the organization's strategic direction. Second, the chair should inspire others to work toward the organization's vision and understand the organization's strengths and weaknesses, as well as the interests of other board members."[10]

Nepotism

Nepotism is a specific form of conflict of interest involving favoritism shown to relatives or friends or associates, including the employment of relatives and the supervision of one relative by another. *Nepotism* policies should define what the organization means by the term, and they should make clear what the prohibited relationships are. For example, consider the following sample statements:

1. Board members and their immediate family members as well as relatives of senior staff members will be excluded from consideration for employment by this organization.

2. Employees shall not hold a position of employment with the organization while they or a family member serves on the board or any committee of the board.

3. Employees may not hold a job or position over which a member of their family exercises supervisory authority. In this section, as well as in sections 1 and 2 above, "family" includes husband, wife, son, son-in-law, daughter, daughter-in-law, father, father-in-law, mother, mother-in-law, brother, brother-in-law, sister, sister-in-law, grandparents, and grandchildren.

Because all policies must reflect the operational realities of the institution, these sample statements may be stricter than necessary. For example, there might be a need for the hospital to employ members of a trustee's family. This can be done with adequate and full disclosure to the board. Alternatively, in some communities with limited resources, a family member can provide expertise that is not easily accessible or available elsewhere in the community. The following case raises this issue in a different context.

Case 5-7. Matrimonial Bliss?

The longstanding chairperson of your board is Mrs. Jefferson Rightfield. She has been chair more than ten years, stepping in when her husband, who had been chair for the preceding ten years, died suddenly of a heart attack. Not only has she increased the level of donations as the years have passed, but she has also been a highly effective chair, streamlining board committees, ensuring that committee work was not duplicated at board meetings, and becoming well educated about the hospital's activities and about health care delivery in general.

Two years ago, the hospital hired a new CEO. Shortly after his arrival, his wife became ill and died. The CEO and Mrs. Rightfield have now announced their plans to marry.

Questions for discussion:

1. Should the board address this conflict of interest? If so, how?
2. What policies should it have in place to guide the hospital in dealing with such problems in the future?

An article by Robert Felton, Alec Hudnut, and Valda Witt in *The McKinsey Quarterly* notes: "Redesigning the governance process to foster a board's independence from management can involve some challenging steps, such as adjusting the composition of the board or establishing formal mechanisms for evaluating its effectiveness."[11] The article contains explicit guidance for carrying out a redesign of the governance process. It includes the following action plans.

Step one: Establish an independent board that works with management but is not controlled by top executives. This can be accomplished by the following actions:

- Form a board governance committee to oversee all board activities.
- Include some outside directors on key committees, such as the audit, governance, and compensation committees.

Step two: Actively determine appropriate board composition and establish membership criteria.

Step three: Run effective, planned board and committee meetings by:

- Using consent agendas
- Sending materials in advance
- Ensuring that trustees are prepared
- Creating opportunities for planned trustee turnover

Step four: Use an ongoing board evaluation system to review performance and obtain feedback on decisions already made and implemented.

Step five: Communicate with numerous stakeholder groups to share information, gather opinions, and field-test ideas.

The following, and final, chapter focuses on creating and implementing policies for an ethical organization. Policies are more than a rigid set of rules: board members must make sure policies are flexible enough that staff members can bend or break them when necessary.

References

1. Sherman, Silverstein, Kohl, Rose, and Podolsky, Complaint/Civil Action, Philadelphia County Court of Common Pleas, Trial Division, Term 2000, www.sskrplaw.com/links/healthcare2.html.
2. R. J. Porter, "Conflict of Interest in Research: The Fundamentals," in R. E. Porter and T. E. Molone, *Biomedical Research: Collaboration and Conflict of Interest* (Baltimore: Johns Hopkins University Press, 1992).
3. B. F. Orlans, T. L. Beauchamp, R. Dresser, D. B. Morton, and J. P. Gluck, *The Human Use of Animals: Case Studies in Ethical Choice* (New York: Oxford University Press, 1998).
4. K. Eichenwald and G. Kolata, "The System: Industry Sees Need to Enlist Doctors," *New York Times,* 30 November 1999.
5. E. Press and J. Washburn, "The Kept University," *Atlantic Monthly* 285, no. 3 (2000): 39–54.
6. E. G. DeRenzo, "Coercion in the Recruitment and Retention of Human Research Subjects, Pharmaceutical Industry Payments to Physician-Investigators, and the Moral Courage of IRB," *IRB: A Review of Human Subjects Research* 22, no. 2 (2000): 1–5.
7. D. Shalala, "Protecting Research Subjects—What Must Be Done?" *New England Journal of Medicine* 343, no. 11 (2000): 808–10.
8. D. F. Thompson, "Understanding Financial Conflicts of Interests," *New England Journal of Medicine* 329, no. 8 (1993): 573–79.
9. J. K. Vincky, S. S. Edwards and J. P. Orlowski, "Conflicts of Interests, Conflicting Interests, and Interesting Conflicts," *Journal of Clinical Ethics* 6, no. 4 (1995): 358–66.
10. P. Hemann, "Build Trust on Your Board," *Board Member* 11, no. 4 (April 2002): 11.
11. R. F. Felton, A. Hudnut, and V. Witt, "Building a Stronger Board," *McKinsey Quarterly* 2 (1995): 164.

6

Conclusions and Actions

THE MOST effective boards, writes Edward Lawler and his colleagues, "have highly knowledgeable directors, the information they need to make decisions and, most important, the power to act."[1] If only this simple statement were so easy to implement in daily practice!

Preparing for Unintended Consequences

Hospital leaders frequently reach for policy decisions when they are addressing an issue that has caused, or has the potential to cause, harm to the institution, its employees, or its patients. But policy decisions may have unanticipated and unintended consequences, and the board should be aware of this and be prepared to address the consequences when appropriate. Trustees should encourage rigorous evaluations of pending policy decisions, which could uncover the potential for unintended consequences.

The following case study raises questions about the unintended consequences of a policy that (probably) had a rational basis. The case also raises questions about irrational and strict adherence to a policy, even when the results of the policy may have been in direct opposition to the mission of the hospital.

Case 6-1. When a Door Becomes a Wall

At a Chicago hospital, a child bled to death because a hospital policy prohibited personnel from going outside the hospital to bring someone into the emergency room. Apparently a young boy was shot while playing basketball. His friends carried him onto the hospital grounds, then ran into the emergency room to get someone to help them get their friend inside. Nobody would go outside to get the boy because it was against hospital policy to do so. By the time the boy's friends went back and finally got him inside, with the help of a police officer, it was too late to save him.

Questions for discussion:

1. What ethical issues are at stake in this situation?
2. How would you recommend this hospital proceed?
3. What policies should the board put in place to guide such decisions in the future?
4. How well is your board prepared to deal with such issues?

The story of this child was reported by major wire services across the country. This case was not necessarily an example of bad policy, but it is the quintessential example of mindless adherence to policy. One can analyze this case from numerous perspectives. Was the emergency room so haphazardly staffed or so chaotically managed that this boy's friends could not make the gravity of their friend's condition understood? Was the ER stretched so thin that the staff members were too burned out to appreciate the severity of the boy's wound? Was the institutional culture so rigid that professionals were afraid to act outside the stated policy? Whatever the reasons, a seemingly rational policy was followed so tightly that a child may have died needlessly. Many factors combined to produce this child's death, but surely one of the most glaring came from the hospital staff members who reported they were following hospital policy.

One can address the appropriateness of a policy that requires a patient to enter the hospital portals before receiving treatment, but that is not the issue for this chapter. For our purposes, let's assume that the policy was sound and that it did, in fact, prohibit ER personnel from going outside the hospital to help bring patients into the emergency room. But as the case of this boy's death suggests, there will be times when following the rules is simply the wrong moral choice.

This case is an excellent example of when professionals should break the rules. Now, some may find these words heretical. Breaking rules can lead to chaos and anarchy, not a state one would advocate for the ethical operation of a hospital. But individuals and committees create rules and policies. There are instances when the rule does not apply as expected or when the policy simply does not adequately fit the circumstances. This case is one such instance.

Recognizing Contradictory Needs

How does a hospital create an environment that encourages staff members to follow well-crafted rules and sound policies while, at the same time, being a place with appropriate responses to unusual circumstances? The hospital can be a place that rewards moral courage and anticipates the need for courageous behavior (with subsequent review). But courage for what? Rather than critically examining the continued value of any particular rule or policy when circumstances call into question its relevance, adherence to the rule can become the goal.

Unfortunately, the old responses can repeat themselves, and staff members may say to the newcomers: "That's how we've always done it" or "That's how it's done here." It takes courage to suggest that an old habit needs changing or that longstanding policies or practices need review. It takes even greater fortitude to suggest that another route needs to be taken. But as the case of the shooting death of the Chicago boy teaches, sometimes there simply isn't time to act cautiously.

What if someone in the emergency room had exclaimed, "I don't care what the policy says, we need to help this boy," and had saved this child's life? It is likely that the staff member would have been applauded for heroic action; it is also possible that he or she might have been chastised for breaking hospital policy. If these two discordant responses had occurred, what might be the effect on the institution? Certainly, one can expect that there would be a further reluctance to perform courageous acts. People behave in ways that organizations support, encourage, and reward. If certain actions are rewarded, there is a great likelihood that an individual will repeat the action. If punished, the behavior is not likely to be repeated.

A hospital needs to be trusted, and part of building trust is to act in ways that are known, knowable, and consistent. Doing so maximizes the possibility that, under normal circumstances, outcomes will be better than they will in a situation that is unpredictable and chaotic. At the same time, however, courageous and heroic tendencies in health care staff members and professionals carry important moral imperatives. For example, courageous health care providers will be more inclined than those with a more laissez-faire attitude to track down family members when an unidentified patient is brought in with an emergency. Heroic staff members speak up and debate with the chief of surgery when a procedure no longer seems to be in the patient's best clinical interest. They will stay to meet with a patient so that another family member can be present. They can be expected to be willing to serve actively rather than perfunctorily on the hospital's ethics committee and ethics consultation service. These are the everyday heroic and courageous acts that lay the foundation for staff members to act responsibly in crisis situations like the one in Chicago.

Fostering Courageous Behavior

How might these two needs—one for order, consistency, and a willingness to follow reasonable procedures and the other for fostering heroic and courageous behavior in staff members—coexist harmoniously?

The board must ensure that processes be established for evaluating inappropriate or dysfunctional policies and procedures. These reviews should exist within a nonpunitive atmosphere of trust and mutual respect for the good judgment of staff members. And nowhere is an institution more inclined to demonstrate its ability to create such a nonpunitive and respectful atmosphere than it is in the role of risk management and legal advisers.

When there is a case in your hospital that requires a difficult decision, who gets called first—someone on the ethics committee or someone in the risk management and legal departments? If it is the latter, there may be a problem. For the most part, risk management and legal departments have existed longer than hospital ethics committees or ethics programs. These committees and programs arose because even though professionals are independently responsible for their own ethical behavior, institutions must create ways to limit corporate liability. We continue to believe that individuals are responsible for making their own ethical judgments, and we now recognize that good persons may disagree, leading to ethically and legally complex situations for both individuals and institutions. How a hospital adjusts to this realization is a clear indicator of whether it creates an environment that fosters courageous behavior or supports an atmosphere of fearfulness and self-protection.

Unlike some authors, we believe the traditional ethics committee is not the best locus for such decisions. Several factors strongly support this conclusion. Primarily, the patient ethics committee is mandated to look at individual doctor-patient relationships. The board, however, needs to work in concert with the CEO to develop a separate organizational ethics structure, process, and conversation. Avoiding issues of organizational policy, governance, and strategy will not resolve conflicts.

Effective Policy Formulation for Ethical Practice

One of the most important roles for all governing boards is to formulate effective policies for their facility. Policies serve as guidelines for the work of the organizational members. Many of these policies emanate from the professional codes of ethics. For example, medicine, nursing, and social work have clear standards and policies about confidentiality. And employees do not need to be told that there is a policy against stealing.

Board members need to assure the community that there are appropriate reinforcements for supporting organizational ethical postulates and the consequences for violating them. Information can come from a variety of perspectives—including financial, medical, legal, and administrative—and patients' perspectives as well.

The following guidelines will assist a board in working with its executive in the development of sound policies:

- Policies must be flexible. Not every organizational and interpersonal situation can be accurately predicted in advance. A policy is not intended to be a rule. It should not eliminate the use of sound, on-the-spot judgments by people acting in the best interest of the facility or the patient. Because flexibility is a desired trait, it follows that reasonable exceptions are tolerable.

- Policies must be acceptable to, and accepted by, the employees who are affected by them. For example, there is little sense in establishing a policy of not leaving the hospital without the director's approval. Such a policy is counterproductive to both the employee (who may have legitimate reasons for leaving) and the director (who almost certainly does not have the time to scrutinize all such requests). Acceptability is strengthened by staff participation in analyzing issues and formulating policies.

- Sound policies should be written and disseminated to all those who are expected to adhere to them. No board or executive should hold an employee accountable for a hidden policy. Although this is obvious, it is sometimes forgotten.

- Sound policies must be internally consistent with other policies and practices in the same organization. For example, if one policy states that "patient records should remain in the hospital," it is not consistent for the hospital to allow selected staff members to take them home regularly for review.

- Effective policies are periodically reviewed. Like the organizational chart, which is seemingly always out of date, so too are many organizational policies. It is the board's responsibility to review and update system policies.

In order for these guidelines to work most effectively, organizations also need a documented, written, and effective dissent process. No system is immune from conflict and tough decisions. Grievance procedures provide protection from abuses and an outlet to address potential concerns and alleged violations. The governing board and top administration must ensure that there are also systemwide avenues for staff members to advocate for better care of all patients, not just the patient in their charge at the moment. Whistle-blowers who advocate for system change should not be condemned for their courageous actions, as they usually are. This is a result of confusing the message of concern with the messenger.

In summary, good policies are like the engines of the Indianapolis race cars. They require tuning and refining. Trustees who pay attention to policy development ensure that actions and deeds remain congruent with mission and strategic plans. This is a prerequisite to a strong ethical organization, and it begins with the individual trustees and the board as an entity.

Strong Ethical Awareness Programs

There is an old axiom that unless we find ethical lapses, there are none. This axiom resulted in a culture of benign neglect, lack of concern, and inattention. Then, when problems emerged, individuals received the blame: "It was Chris Smith's fault that this happened." Strong institutions understand that ethical concerns are part of their daily responsibilities. These are just as important as complying with the current fire laws. Inaction does not encourage people to act in a fair, equitable, and positive manner. It only says: use your judgment and all will be fine.

But history tells a different story. Fewer ethical violations, enhanced risk management programs, possibly reduced liability insurance premiums (like a defensive driving course), increased pride, and an established pattern of positive action are all demonstrable benefits of greater ethical awareness on the part of employees. Human resource departments should be conducting a wide variety of training activities, emphasizing practice skills, managerial needs, financial realities, new policies, and legal changes. Ethical decision making and standards should be on the agenda for all employees, not just for new staff members.

Ultimately, operational issues should be delegated to the chief executive officer, and rightly so. But the board of trustees must ensure that ethical issues are comprehensively, systematically, and routinely brought to the fore. One way for health care organizations to respond is to develop a systemwide ethical awareness program. The benefits of activities in such a program are important to the organization. They provide staff members with information about the issues they will confront in their work. Pamphlets, speakers, brown-bag luncheon discussions, ethical grand rounds, and newsletters can provide opportunities for case discussions. Such public conversations empower staff members who see potential problems to come forward because the culture supports such behavior. Some people might have the misperception that ethics training indicates numerous ethical problems. If that logic were taken to its unacceptable extreme, no ethical problem would ever be reported.

Libraries are filled with decision-making models. Most of them assume that the process is linear, beginning with a problem statement that leads to data collection, analysis, choice, implementation, and assessment. But rarely does the process work so simply and in such a straightforward manner. For example, a common statement such as "we need more funds to continue our clinic hours" is not a problem statement; in fact, it defines a solution. Depending on the specific case, a problem statement could read: "How do we meet the increased demand for outpatient services?" Although funds may be part of a possible solution, they are not the only solution.

A problem statement defines the process and the discussion. An *efficient* process may drive out dissent in the search for action, whereas an *effective* process creates choices and explores reasonable differences. Because policy decisions often reflect differences in values and perspectives, effective actions must be grounded in board consensus. Actions taken with only a 51 percent majority will likely run into trouble. Better solutions exist but only if the board devotes the time needed to search for them.

Much of the board's work is done in committees. Clearly this serves the valuable purpose of delegating tasks to increase the board's overall efficiency. Smaller groups can delve into details that the entire board doesn't want to consider. Trustees can develop special expertise in one or two critical aspects of the organization's operations. And committees can let boards test ideas before they are fully formulated.

But efficiency may detract from effectiveness. The traditional practice of board work is to have an issue debated in committee. Then at the formal board meeting, the chair of the working group presents the issue and the committee's recommendation. Discussion ensues, the vote is taken, and the board moves on to another agenda item. For this process to work, each board committee *must* specify the value conflicts as they emerge. Expanding clinic hours, for example, pits increased cost against community need. Questions of a cost-benefit analysis emerge, but these are not all objective, quantifiable, and rational. This is where the organization's mission statement can provide guidance.

We propose a modest change to enhance the board's conversation and education. In addition to defining a proposed course of action, the committee chair and its members should also present an option or two, which they may choose not to recommend. Not only will this presentation explain and support their proposed position on the issue, but it will also educate and enlighten the other members of the board. As more information is shared, the effectiveness of the board increases.

Building a Strong Board for Tomorrow—Today!

The stakes are real and expensive. As most hospitals know, the federal sentencing guidelines have become the catalyst for health care organizations to develop a comprehensive organizational ethics program. Never being vague about the cost of noncompliance, the public law gives a 95 percent waiver of penalty if the institution has an effective plan and program in place. In order for this to occur, however, the board must take several steps periodically, as indicated within each of the following steps:

- The board must review and update the organizational mission statement (perhaps every five to seven years).

- The board must promulgate a clear statement of organizational values and principles (annually).
- The board must form a group of key members to serve as the organizational ethics team (OET) (ongoing).
- The board must provide ample resources for the OET to plan, offer, and assess educational programs (annually).
- The board must ensure the continuing education of the OET's members (annually).
- The board must rotate OET membership periodically (on a planned basis).
- The board must evaluate the OET's work (annually).
- The board must publish (print, Web, and so on) an organizational ethics summary (annually).

In closing, we hope the ideas and approaches in this volume stimulate discussion and compel trustees to take action. Lethargy and ignorance are no longer acceptable excuses or defenses. They harm the institution, its service, and—most important—its patients, clients, and the general public. Those are the specific groups that trustees have a fiduciary responsibility to serve.

Reference

1. E. E. Lawler III, D. Finegold, G. Benson, and J. Conger, "Adding Value in the Boardroom," *MIT Sloan Management Review* 43, no. 2 (Winter 2002): 92.

Index